Who is this Man?

Man?

Christ in the Renewal of the Church

Edited by William Davage and
Jonathan Baker

continuum
LONDON • NEW YORK

Continuum UK
The Tower Building
11 York Road
London SE1 7NX

Continuum US
80 Maiden Lane
Suite 704
New York, NY 10038

www.continuumbooks.com

First published 2006

British Library Cataloguing-in-Publication Data
A catalogue record for this book is available from the British Library.

ISBN 0–8264–8157–4

Lyrics from Joy © Jagger courtesy of WarnerChappell Music Ltd.
Lyrics from Grace © U2
Lyrics from *Every Grain of Sand* © Bob Dylan
Lyrics from *I Don't Know How to Love Him* © Lloyd-Webber/Rice courtesy Universal Music Publishing
Lyrics from *Ties that Bind, Human Touch* and *the Rising* © Springsteen

Typeset in Monotype Bembo by Servis Filmsetting Limited, Manchester
Printed and bound by Antony Rowe Ltd, Chippenham, Wilts.

Contents

Preface

Jonathan Baker

The Society of the Holy Cross gathered for its celebrations and conference in April 2005 seeking renewal in its priesthood through prayer, worship and study. The Theological Conference was preceded by an International Synod of the Society held at St Alban the Martyr, Holborn and concluded with a note of triumph at the Royal Albert Hall when over seven hundred priests concelebrated and five thousand people attended Mass.

The theme of the Conference was the High Priesthood of Jesus Christ, the ministerial priesthood of the ordained, and the royal priesthood of all the baptized, and the relationship and interplay among all three. It is of course true that in the New Testament we find only the high priesthood of Jesus Christ and the priesthood of all the baptized, the priesthood of the whole priestly people of God. The ministerial priesthood is derived from Christ's priesthood, and is at the service of the priestly people of God. It is given to enable the priestly vocation of the whole Church. It is both distinct from the priesthood of the whole body, and at the service of the priesthood of the whole body.

Professors David Brown and Ann Loades reflected on the person of Our Lord Jesus Christ, the high priest, crucified and risen for us. Both are well known for their work on Christianity and the arts. They gave two lively and distinctive presentations with a wealth of visual material and musical extracts. They sought to convey, through this variety of media, the developing perception of Our Lord's suffering, death and resurrection from early medieval to modern times. It is impossible in a purely printed form to realize their unique blend of the visual and the aural. However, they have very kindly undertaken to adapt their lectures for this book, so that those reading their material should experience no sense of loss of their insights and argument.

The Conference took place as the world mourned the passing of Pope John Paul II and awaited the election of his successor. We were therefore deeply grateful to the Archbishop of Canterbury for fulfilling his commitment to the Society amidst the extraordinary and unprecedented events happening in Rome, to where he travelled immediately after delivering his lecture. He also was generous with his time by taking a number of questions, which form part of his contribution to this book. His reflections through the Psalms on the priesthood, and on the Son of God as the one who alone offers fitting worship to the Father, spoke keenly and directly to the priests of the Society.

The Bishop of Guildford and Dr Mary Tanner spoke on different aspects of the call to unity as part of our priestly mission, drawing on their long and detailed experience of ecumenical dialogue and discussion. Their lectures touched, inevitably, on matters of contemporary concern to Catholics in the Church of England, and provided much material for mature reflection and some lively discussion at the Conference.

In addition to these substantial theological contributions to the Conference, this book makes available the texts of sermons, meditations and devotional addresses which were given during the worship which sustained and nourished the delegates during the course of the week-long celebrations. They are representative of the heart and soul of the Catholic Revival, as it is now lived and experienced in the Church of England today by the heirs of the leaders of the Oxford Movement. Their values – the sacramental life, the vocation to personal holiness, the sanctification of the world and the unity of the whole Church of God – remain as vital now as they were then.

The Society of the Holy Cross hopes that this book will make a lasting contribution to the pursuit, under God, and in the Sign of the Cross, of the Catholic Faith as the Church of England has received it, and as she seeks to proclaim it afresh to each generation.

In Hoc Signo Vinces

Editorial Notes

As noted in the Preface, the Conference took place in the week of the funeral of Pope John Paul II and this greatly influenced, and was reflected in, the tone and the substance of the contributions made. Unfortunately Cardinal Cormac Murphy-O'Connor, the Archbishop of Westminster, was unable to fulfil his engagement but the Archbishop of Canterbury was able to deliver his address before leaving for Rome to attend the funeral.

Most references to the Pope's death and the importance of his pontificate have been retained to indicate the particular flavour and context of the Conference.

We have aimed to exercise only the lighest editorial touch and have sought to retain something of the spontaneity of the spoken word, but we have shaped more extensively those contributions which were transcribed from the tape recordings of the Conference and which were delivered without a full written text.

At the International Synod of the Society of the Holy Cross which opened the week of celebration for its one hundred and fiftieth anniversary on Tuesday, 5 April 2005, the Rt Revd Dr Geoffrey Rowell, Bishop of Gibraltar in Europe and the newly appointed Visitor to the Society, gave a lecture on the history of the Society in its context. This appears in the companion volume, *In This Sign Conquer: a History of the Society of the Holy Cross 1855–2005* (London, 2006).

Jonathan Baker and William Davage

Acknowledgements

The editorial task was greatly helped by the cooperation of the contributors and their prompt delivery of their lectures, addresses and sermons.

The Conference was recorded and we are grateful to Catherine Hoar for transcribing the tapes.

Our colleague on the Chapter of Pusey House, Fr Barry Orford, the Archivist, was, as usual, encouraging, generous with his time, helpful and constructively critical in equal measure.

Contributors

The Revd Jonathan Baker SSC is Principal of Pusey House, Oxford.

The Revd Professor David Brown is Van Mildert Professor of Theology in the University of Durham.

The Rt Revd Andrew Burnham SSC is Bishop of Ebbsfleet.

The Revd William Davage SSC is Priest Librarian and Custodian of the Library, Pusey House, Oxford.

The Rt Revd Christopher Hill is Bishop of Guildford.

The Revd Prebendary David Houlding SSC is the Vicar of All Hallows' Gospel Oak and is the Master-General of the Society of the Holy Cross. From 1995 to 2005 he was also the Provincial Master of England and Scotland.

Professor Ann Loades is Professor Emerita of Theology in the University of Durham.

The Rt Revd Keith Newton SSC is Bishop of Richborough.

The Revd Philip North is the Administrator of the Shrine of Our Lady of Walsingham.

The Rt Revd Paul Richardson SSC is Assistant Bishop in the Diocese of Newcastle.

The Revd Dr Jeremy Sheehy SSC is Principal of St Stephen's House, Oxford.

The Revd Dr Andrew Sloane SSC is Rector of St Paul's, Washington DC.

The Revd Canon Barry Swain SSC is Rector of the Church of the Resurrection, New York City.

Dr Mary Tanner is sometime Secretary of the Council for Christian Unity.

The Revd Dr Robin Ward SSC is the Vicar of St John the Baptist, Sevenoaks and Canon Theologian of Rochester Cathedral.

The Revd Dr Martin Warner SSC is Canon Pastor of St Paul's Cathedral, London.

The Most Revd and Rt Hon. Dr Rowan Williams is Archbishop of Canterbury.

1

To What End Are We Made?

The Archbishop of Canterbury

The old catechisms tell us that we are made by God to know him, to love him, to serve him and to be happy with him for ever. 'In thy presence is the fullness of life', says the Psalmist. We are made so that we shall reflect back to God the glory that belongs to God. We are made to hold up to God a mirror to who he is and what he is. We are most truly our created selves when we are thus living in the imaging of God, in relating to God. As God is truly himself, truly who and what he is, in being freely and gladly for us, so we are fully ourselves when we freely relate in love to him. That is what we are for. And it is a point that has been laboured often enough, but is perhaps worth making again, that in a world where we are not very sure, corporately, what we are for, it is all the more important for the Church to know precisely what we are for, why we are made. It is important for the Church to say that we have a destiny, and that destiny is the enjoyment of God: the enjoyment of God is the fullness of our life and our identity. Our destiny is that adoration of God which holds up before him who he is and what he is, as the image that he has implanted in us grows to its fulfilment and fruition.

We are ourselves when we reflect God to God. And, of course, that reflection is partly in action towards one another in the life of charity, of selflessness, which God requires of us in our relations one with another. But, crucially, it is also about reflecting God directly. Moses spoke with God as a man speaks with his

1

friend', face to face. So we may be fully human in God's purpose, in our love for the world, in the charity drawn out of us by God's grace, in our relations with one another especially in the body of Christ; but we shall not be fully human if our love for the world is all there is to it. We are fully human in the contemplation of God's eternal mystery and the joy that comes with that.

So, what we are made for is worship. And central to the Christian gospel is that proclamation. Worship is our destiny. Worship is our joy and our fruition. As I reflected on the question of the priesthood of Christ, it came to me that one could construct a meditation on the subject almost entirely out of the Psalms. And so I want to punctuate my own meditations with some of the words of the Psalms. And you might like to think for a moment of this opening notion of our destiny being worship in and through the words of Psalm 63:

> O God, thou art my God : early will I seek thee.
> My soul thirsteth for thee, my flesh also longeth after thee : in a barren and dry land where no water is.
> Thus have I looked for thee in holiness : that I might behold thy power and glory.
> For thy loving-kindness is better than the life itself : my lips shall praise thee.
> As long as I live will I magnify thee on this manner : and lift up my hands in thy Name. (Ps. 63.1–5)

If our end is worship, and if our charity towards one another springs from and is inseparably bound up with that worship, we begin to understand, perhaps, that sin is not simply the refusal or failure of charity between us sin is also the refusal of worship. Sin is what leads to an incapacity for worship. And if it leads to an incapacity for worship, it leads to an incapacity for love. Where does sin begin? In scripture it begins with somebody listening all too sympathetically to the seductive suggestion that you can be 'as gods'. In other words, you need have no one to worship. Sin begins in the lie that worship is an unwelcome obligation, and that to be freely ourselves is to be liberated from worship. But this then means that making peace with God, the overcoming of sin, is the restoration of the capacity for worship: the full acknowledgement that God is God. Within that acknowledgement is a recognition, not that we owe God some immense debt of worship, although that language is sometimes understandably used, but much more importantly that it is in worship that we live. If we refuse to worship, we choose death. To refuse to worship is *not* to become like gods; it is to become less than human. So it is that, if we turn yet again to the Psalms, the hope of the penitent is not only for absolution, it is for integration into the community of worship.

> Thou shalt open my lips, O Lord : and my mouth shall shew thy praise.
> For thou desirest no sacrifice, else would I give it thee : but thou delightest not in burnt-offerings.
> The sacrifice of God is a troubled spirit : a broken and contrite heart, O God, shalt thou not despise.
> O be favourable and gracious unto Sion : build thou the walls of Jerusalem.
> Then shalt thou be pleased with the sacrifice of righteousness, with the burnt-offerings and oblations : then shall they offer young bullocks upon thine altar. (Ps. 51.15–19)

And in Psalm 43 we hear:

> O send out thy light and thy truth, that they may lead me : and bring me unto thy holy hill, and to thy dwelling.
> And that I may go unto the altar of God, even unto the God of my joy and gladness: and upon the harp will I give thanks unto thee, O God, my God. (Ps. 43.3–4)

The overcoming of alienation is in the same moment, at one and the same time, an entry into the fullness of worship. And so in scripture the Law of Moses does not simply prescribe our behaviour towards one another, the Law gathers human beings into a *people*: a coherent community capable of acting as one. In the process of making peace with the God whose worship has been refused, one figure acts for them in the process of peace-making. The cost of leaving behind self-interest and returning to God, the paradoxical cost involved in re-acquainting ourselves with the joy for which we were made, is symbolized by a costly gift, a token of surrender or letting go. That is to say, in the Law priests offer sacrifices on behalf of the people, a costly gift is made, whose effect is peace. Not only does the priest offer on behalf of the people, the priest's task is also to offer the people God's gift in consequence of the peace that has been made. The sacrifice is offered, received and then shared. Here is St Thomas Aquinas on the subject:

> The proper job of the priest is to be a mediator between God and the people. In that he gives divine things to the people, and again in that he offers the people's prayers to God and in some sense makes reparation to God for the people's sins.[1]

He gives divine things to the people. Not only does he offer, make peace through sacrifice, he distributes and realizes the consequences of that peace. Sin is addressed, then, not by a word of absolution alone, not by human acts of reparation directed individually towards a distant God; sin is overcome and dealt with by the restoration of the capacity to worship: to acknowledge God, to give to God that gift which makes us most fully free, most fully human. This of course is where in the New Testament era the great transition, the great recognition, happens. All that has been said so far remains at the level of symbol or of figure. It is human action taken to repair a bond that is always broken, temporarily restored and broken again. As the writer of the letter to the Hebrews insists, these are sacrifices that never get to the root of our refusal of worship. As the New Testament suggests, this is a process which can even intensify our fear, or our anxiety. Have we done enough? Have we given enough? Have we satisfied?

Peace itself is the giving of self to God. Who among us is free to give ourselves to God? Because all of us are affected by the refusal to give and to worship, that ingrained habit of refusal frustrates, distorts, derails the peacemaking process again and again. Who is free from that ingrained refusal of worship? Ultimately the answer can only be the same one who first gives life to all. God is free and God alone is free to image God perfectly to God.

God alone – what a strange thing this is to say – God alone is free to worship. That is to say, God is free to reflect a perfect gift in perfect love and gratitude. God alone is free to rejoice in perfect selflessness at a perfect bestowal of life. Whether we are looking at Hebrews or at Colossians the New Testament is clear: only the first-born of God is free in this way, free with God's own freedom, therefore free with God's own love, therefore the paradigm, the heart of all worship.

It is a paradox. It sounds very odd to our ears to say God alone can worship. Yet what worship means is a joyful reflection of a gift without defensiveness or fear. That is a liberty that belongs to the Creator alone in its fullness. 'I am ascending', says Jesus to Mary Magdalene, 'to my Father and your Father, to my God and your God' (John 20.17) Many of the commentators of the early Church make the point that in some sense when Jesus uses those words, speaking of his Father not only as his Father but as God, he stands as the perfect worshipper of God, the one who does not snatch at equality with God, but reflects and responds in full perfection to the gift that has been given: that is how the argument of the Letter to the Hebrews unfolds in all its complexity and tormented intellectual majesty. It is not an easy letter to read, but the essence of the argument in Hebrews lies there. Who but the first-born is able to make peace by renewing in us the liberty of worship? If Christ has cut to the very root of our refusal of worship, then the work of Christ is about equipping us for worship. Christ, in restoring the image of God in us, precisely restores the capacity for worship. That is why the very heart of the gift of Christ's spirit to the Church lies in our being set free to address God as Father. We need to read Galatians 4 and Romans 8 alongside the Letter to the Hebrews:

> God has sent the Spirit of his Son into our hearts, crying 'Abba, Father'. (Gal. 4.6)

If Christ has done this, if Christ has transformed our capacity for worship, carved out a place for us to stand, of which before we knew nothing, it must be because his is a freedom beyond ours. The very first recognition of the full implications of the divine lordship of Christ, in the New Testament era, is bound to him inseparably with the priority of finding a new way of prayer in him. It is because Jesus teaches us and equips us to say 'Our Father' that we begin to know who Jesus is. We are able to be for God, as we were made to be because God has been fully for us in Jesus. And God's very being for us in Jesus is the outworking of his purpose that we should be for him in his own love and contemplation: not just by the setting of an example but by the creating of something new in us.

> I waited patiently for the Lord : and he inclined unto me, and heard my calling.
> He brought me also out of the horrible pit, out of the mire and clay : and set my feet upon the rock, and ordered my goings.
> And he hath put a new song in my mouth : even a thanksgiving unto our God. . . .
> Sacrifice, and meat-offering, thou wouldest not : but mine ears hast thou opened.
> Burnt-offerings, and sacrifice for sin, hast thou not required : then said I, Lo, I come,
> In the volume of the book it is written of me, that I should fulfil thy will, O my God : I am content to do it; yea, thy law is within my heart.
> I have declared thy righteousness in the great congregation[.]
> (Ps. 40.1–3, 8–11a)

Psalm 40 echoes through the pages of the Letter to the Hebrews, and is perhaps at its most poignant and meaningful when recited during the Triduum. Mercy and truth are not withheld, they are communicated to the great assembly of God's people. Through the obedience of Christ we are all set free. So the perfect offering of peace is made. What is offered to God is our human nature, but who it is offered by is God. It is the central mystery of our faith, the essential balance of the teaching of the Council of Chalcedon. I am very impatient with those who think that the Council of Chalcedon and its definition are remote technicalities. They are our lifeblood because the words that were there agreed by the Spirit's guidance, so we trust, are words that express precisely this mystery. It is God who offers worship to God, and yet for that to be something transformative of our human nature, it must be human nature that is offered by God to God. It is a humanity absolutely like ours, offered by a purpose and an energy absolutely unlike ours.

It works at two levels at least. Christ in his offering of obedience, and the culmination of that offering on the Cross, breaks through the historic impossibility of human self-offering to God, breaks through, is free from, the entail of sin. That inherited impossibility in human life of worshipping fully and freely is overcome once and for all. Where Adam refused worship because he wanted to be like a god, Christ does not consider equality with God as a thing to be snatched or hoarded and, therefore, restores the possibility of worship and of joy to human creatures. Christ in his dying makes something possible. But that possibility is made actual, made real, because his humanity is not simply that of a distant individual, it is a humanity inclusive of our very nature as a whole. It becomes more than an individual life. In baptism it is Christ's breath that we breathe. By his life we live, when we are baptized. In the Eucharist the gift of his Body and Blood means that we are associated with, drawn into the agency, the energy of, his humanity, penetrated as it is by the action of God.

When we say that the life and death of Jesus Christ restores a possibility to the human world we do not stop there. We go on to say that that possibility is made real when the humanity of Christ takes in our own, when his Spirit is communicated to us so our life becomes his, when his Body and Blood take root in us and we live more deeply into his life. When at every Mass we return into the baptismal identity that we all share, and that of course is part of what the Eucharist is, it is reclaiming our identity as baptized people, as people in Christ; when that happens, to paraphrase a turn of phrase of a modern Romanian Orthodox writer, 'the prayers of Christians become the prayer of the Church' and our particular aspirations and hopes, our particular intercessions and petitions, are drawn into Christ's eternal self-giving to the Father, that self-giving which is always there on our behalf in the Christ who lives for ever to make intercession for

7

us. That is the sense of the great words of St Augustine: you are on the altar; you are in the cup, in the Eucharist.[2]

When we understand what it is that we are affirming when we confess Jesus Christ to be truly God and truly human we understand something about the nature of our worship that we could not otherwise see. The priesthood of Christ is completely bound up with our acknowledgement of the person of Christ; the divinity of Christ as a person; the reality of the humanity that he offers.

> I am well pleased : that the Lord hath heard the voice of my prayer;
> That he hath inclined his ear unto me : therefore will I call upon him as long as I live. . . .
> What reward shall I give unto the Lord : for all the benefits that he hath done unto me?
> I will receive the cup of salvation : and call upon the Name of the Lord.
> I will pay my vows now in the presence of all his people : right dear in the sight of the Lord is the death of his saints.
> Behold, O Lord, how that I am thy servant : I am thy servant, and the son of thine handmaid; thou hast broken my bonds in sunder.
> I will offer to thee the sacrifice of thanksgiving : and will call upon the Name of the Lord. (Ps. 116.1–2, 11–16)

One of the most significant points we need to recover in our teaching and our witness is precisely what we do and do not say about our worship. If we are not clear in what we say about worship we should not be surprised if our perception of Christ goes badly wrong. In a magnificent essay on the vicarious humanity of Christ by the Scottish Reformed theologian James Torrance written in 1981 as part of the commemorative celebrations of the Council of Constantinople in 381, he begins by identifying two different views of worship in the Church today:

> As I see it there are broadly two different views of worship in the Church today. The first view, probably the most common and widespread, is that worship is something which we do mainly in church

on Sunday. We go to church, we sing our psalms to God, we inter-
cede for Northern Ireland or the Middle East, we listen to the
sermon, too often simply exhortation. We offer our money, time and
talents to God. No doubt we need God's grace to help us do it. We
do it because Jesus taught us to do it and left us an example of how
to do it, but worship is what we do. In theological language this
means that the only priesthood is our priesthood, the only offering
our offering, the only intercessions our intercessions. Indeed this
view of worship is in practice Unitarian, has no doctrine of the
mediator, of the sole priesthood of Christ; is man-centred with no
proper doctrine of the Holy Spirit and is basically non-sacramental
and can engender weariness. We sit in the pew watching the minister doing his thing exhorting us to do our thing, until we go home
thinking we have done our duty for another week.[3]

The second view of worship is that worship is rather the gift
of participating through the Spirit in the incarnate Son's communion with the Father; of participating in union with Christ
in what he has done for us once and for all in his life and death
on the Cross and in what he is continuing to do for us in the
presence of the Father and in his mission to the world. 'The cup
of blessing which we bless, is it not our sharing in the blood of
Christ? The bread which we break, is it not our sharing in the
body of Christ?' (1 Cor. 10.16) Our sonship and communion
with the Father, are they not our sharing by the spirit of adop-
tion in Christ's sonship and communion with the Father? Our
intercessions for Northern Ireland and the Middle East, are they
not our participation in Christ's intercession for Northern
Ireland and the Middle East? Our mission to the world and ministry to the needs of men, are they not the gift of participating
in Christ's mission to the world and his ministry to the needs of
men? Is this not the meaning of life in the Spirit?

If we are not clear about this, very funny things happen to
our doctrine of Christ. Historically of course, funny things *have*
happened. There has been at times a distancing of Christ in God,
a pushing-away of Christ towards God so that we need to work
hard for access to that distant God. We become tied up with

9

the whole system of supplementary mediation. That is what the Reformers rightly discerned as one of the things wrong with medieval Catholicism. Equally though, we can absorb Christ into our humanity so that we fail to see that there is any gift in Christ, any newness, anything in the Church that is actually truly supernatural. It is probably still that second area that is the bigger problem for us at the moment. In many of our current debates in the Church the underlying issue is often whether or not we believe the Church is a supernatural reality. That is a truth which is forgotten almost as much by would-be traditionalists as by self-styled liberals. If we believe that in Christ a new creation, a new humanity is given and if we believe that that is what the Church exists to embody and witness to, it does not answer our specific questions about the debates of the day but it gives us a highly significant framework in which to think them through because it reminds us of two things that we readily lose sight of. One is that the Church is not simply a body that exists to determine its own priorities and its own truth, because it exists by God's gift and, therefore, by the objectivity of what God is actually like and what God has actually done. Equally, it reminds us of the risks of supposing that the unity of the Church is a construct laboriously built up by consensus and like-mindedness among human beings. That is a problem which can afflict traditionalists and liberals alike.

Catholic Christian orthodoxy has held always that our worship is our participation in Christ – not an extra, not an outward expression of some inner conversion. It is being in Christ. When we stand as the community of the baptized praying the Church's prayer in Christ, we are not encouraging ourselves to do something else, or expressing a reality that exists somewhere else; we are where we should be. ' 'Tis a gift to be simple, 'tis a gift to be free, 'tis a gift to come down where you ought to be', says the old Shaker song, and the gift to come down where we ought to be is what is happening in our worship, and, above all, in our Eucharistic worship. We have come down where we ought to be. Where we ought to be is before the throne of God, clothed with Christ, breathing the life of the Spirit. The Eastern

Orthodox are quite right to say, in a sense, that there is nothing else to do, there is nothing else to say. When you are in the midst of the liturgy you are in heaven. The fact that this is probably not the first reaction of many routine Anglican worshippers, or indeed worshippers in many traditions and possibly not even all Orthodox, is something which ought to give us pause for thought and prayer and penitence. Unless we have that straight we have no right to be surprised if people run off into strange and pinched and narrow doctrines of Christ. The two things, perhaps, which are the deepest motors of true belief about Christ are worship and mission. And that should not surprise us in the least. When those motors dry up, we atrophy, are paralyzed; people stop seeing why it is important to confess one God, Father, Son and Holy Spirit, and one Lord complete in two natures. Which is why this is not an academic extra, not an unnecessary complication; it is, or it ought to be, an exhilarating truth: in the most literal sense possible, the truth that makes us happy.

To speak of orthodoxy as a truth that makes us happy is not always the first phrase that might come to mind because we have, sadly, come to think of orthodox belief as a set of obligations to sign up to, rather than as a landscape to inhabit with constant amazement and delight at the discovery opened up. If we understand what the priesthood of Christ means, means for our worship, for our own priesthood too, then we shall have some sense of why orthodox belief is truth that makes us happy.

God's truth is a truth designed to make us happy. You may think God's truth can in many circumstances, for many of us, be something with which we struggle, something which demands of us what we thought we could not give, which keeps our noses to the most uncomfortable grindstones day after day, which leads us to risk, sometimes to humiliation. God's truth is like that, and is it a truth which makes us happy? Yes, because God is bliss. God's nature is bliss. God enjoys God, and that unimaginable interchange of love, gift and delight that is the life of Father, Son and Holy Spirit simply is the way God is. When God makes a world God makes that world so that it may have some share in

11

some degree in that bliss. The truth of how God is is a truth that makes us happy.

If we can proclaim that worship is God's act first then we shall know how to think of Jesus and how to think of ourselves and our eternal destiny. We shall know that in our ministry and all our witness what we have to contend with in God's name is, in various ways and under various disguises, a refusal and an incapacity to worship. How very different some of our mission would look if we said that the main problem with the fallen human race is its incapacity for joy. Yet, if we look at our contemporary world we may understand some of the ways in which that is true. Where but in this eternal relationship of worship is there joy, lasting joy?

> Preserve me, O God : for in thee have I put my trust.
> O my soul, thou hast said unto the Lord : Thou art my God, my goods are nothing unto thee.
> All my delight is upon the saints, that are in the earth : and upon such as excel in virtue.
> But they that run after another god : shall have great trouble.
> Their drink-offerings of blood will I not offer : neither make mention of their names within my lips.
> The Lord himself is the portion of mine inheritance, and of my cup : thou shalt maintain my lot.
> The lot is fallen unto me in a fair ground : yea, I have a goodly heritage.
> I will thank the Lord for giving me warning : my reins also chasten me in the night-season.
> I have set God always before me : for he is on my right hand, therefore I shall not fall.
> Wherefore my heart was glad, and my glory rejoiced : my flesh also shall rest in hope.
> For why? thou shalt not leave my soul in hell : neither shalt thou suffer thy Holy One to see corruption.
> Thou shalt show me the path of life; in thy presence is the fullness of joy : and at thy right hand there is pleasure for evermore.
> (Psalm 16)

Discussion

The Revd Dr Jeremy Sheehy:

I am fascinated by the way in which what you have said to us today picks up themes you have developed elsewhere. Indeed, I think you have given a sort of introduction to the theology of Archbishop Rowan Williams. For instance, we asked you to say something about the priesthood of Christ. You mentioned the Council of Chalcedon, and you have contributed much to the study of that council: a contribution which will be of continuing value is your book on Arius, in which you show the bold, even audacious nature of the theology of Athanasius, whilst Arius is to be seen as a conservative scholar but enabled to rethink the categories of divinity and humanity in the light of the mighty acts of salvation.

I hope you have not fallen into the trap named by Professor Stuart Hall when he says that modern theologians have read into Arianism whatever views they themselves particularly abominate. I do not think you have. First, I know that you are not the sort of theologian who abominates views anyway, because you listen and draw things from them. Secondly, because another major point in your book is that Arianism is not a category that the Church of the fourth century would have recognized, but is a subsequent construct. The relevance of this for our consideration of the priesthood of Christ is that Arius, and the theology on which he built, was prone to make the sonship of Jesus Christ, the ground of his mediation and, therefore, of his priesthood. That is the great error, that is precisely why Arius was so wrong. It is because Jesus Christ, who is of one substance with the Father, is incarnate of one substance also with us, that he is our mediator. The Nicene theology will insist, when developed, that it is the Incarnation that is the ground of his mediation and, therefore, of his priesthood. And the priestly role of Christ emphasizes his incarnation, as you made clear. Perhaps it is the only term of the threefold work of prophet, priest and king that does so strongly and emphatically depend upon the Incarnation. The conflicts around Arius teach us that you cannot satisfactorily guard the transcendence of the

Father by limiting the divinity of the Son and you cannot locate the priesthood of the Son in his sonship rather than in the Incarnation. This leads into some of the themes you illuminate in your study of Teresa of Avila in the series 'Outstanding Christian Thinkers'. You emphasize there the importance of the Incarnation to Teresa, commenting on a theology that lays special stress upon God's desire to be present with the creation. And again on Teresa's account that there is no detached divine absolute with which to take refuge. We meet God wearing the human face of Jesus Christ.

You said that worship is our destiny, our joy and fruition. Worship, of course, equals worth-ship, which might be why refusal truly to worship has the nature of sin. When you preached at Evensong in St Patrick's Cathedral in Armagh, at the time of the meeting of primates in February [2005], you preached on the priesthood of Christ. Your text there was, 'you shall be to me a kingdom of priests and a holy nation' (Exod. 19.6). These words are spoken to the people of Israel, and again, of course, to the Church in the New Testament (1 Pet. 2.9). As you suggested to us, you also suggested there that the priest gives God on behalf of the world to make peace a token of that letting go. Human beings alone could not make lasting peace and so the calling of God's priestly people is summarized and fulfilled in the sending and calling of the one who is our priest, Jesus Christ, the priest for ever after the order of Melchisedek. Here symbol becomes flesh. You went on to say that the Church is above all a place where prayer and supplication and thanksgiving happen. If the Church fails to be such a place, it is no real Church. No one who knows you can fail to realize how important that centrality of prayer and worship is for you.

When I was reading the obituary in *The Times* for Pope John Paul II, with this conference already in my mind and with the transferred celebration of the Annunciation also in my mind, I noticed the comment that the Pope's concept of, and commitment to, what the obituary writer called Catholic humanism depended on the dignity of human beings made in the image of God. I thought, as I read it – and listening to you today has reinforced my reaction – that is true and good as far as it goes but it is desperately incomplete as an account if you stop as *The Times* obituary did there. You must surely add that this dignity of human beings depends on our being made in the image of God, and also on the coming of God imaged in our likeness, come among us in our humanity so that we can say with Bishop Michael Ramsey, 'God is Christlike and in him is no un-Christlikeness'. Or with Bishop David Jenkins in one of his early books, 'God is and is as he is in Jesus, and therefore there is room for hope.'[4] What we are for relates to our bearing the image of God and God's taking our human nature.

The priesthood of Christ depends on his humanity; it also depends, for the New Testament writers, on his sinless humanity. Granted that the ministerial priesthood is not simply about the imitation of Christ, nonetheless, the high priestly prayer in John 17 establishes continuity between Jesus' mission and the mission of the apostles. I find myself wondering what the need for his sinlessness as the ground of the priesthood of Christ has to say to me.

The Archbishop:

That helped me understand what I am saying. I was very delighted that you picked up both the patristic resonances of what I have been saying, but also the way in which for Teresa of Avila the humanity of Christ is not something which we have got to get beyond if we really want to be first-class mystics. Teresa challenges any notion of spiritual maturation that takes us beyond the reality of that divine and human life which is Christ's – for the simple reason that, of course, our prayer is brought into the life of the Trinity by, and only by, that incarnate life and its continuation in the heavenly places.

In response to the last point that was made: the point is exactly right. The notion of Christ's priesthood depends not only on a belief in Christ's humanity, in Christ's solidarity with us; it does depend on Christ's sinlessness. It depends on the idea that here is someone who is free from that crippling taint that makes us incapable of giving ourselves as we are made to do. What that says to us

– who in a very particular and public way not only participate in Christ's priesthood, which is in the Church, but also actualize the priesthood of the Church in a certain mode and in certain contexts – is that one of our constant priestly obligations is to examine our own freedom for, and capacity for, worship, which also means examining those ways in which we occasionally get ourselves and God mixed up together. It means, therefore, that the strange paradoxical truth about priesthood is that we often most effectively let the priesthood of Christ come through in our ministry when we are most clearly and courageously penitent about the ways we do not let it come through. If, in von Hügel's great words, 'the greatest good for unfallen humanity is innocence, the greatest good for fallen humanity is forgiveness', then the greatest good for fallen and sinful priests, that is us, is a habit of repentance. That is the way in which the sinlessness of Christ, paradoxically, plays into our own ministry.

The Revd Dr Robin Ward:

I would like to return briefly to the theme of Christ as the perfect worshipper and to talk a little bit about the Western tradition, in particular the post-Reformation French tradition, and your emphasis on the humanity of Christ as the perfect adorer, the perfect worshipper of the Father, because in the sacrifice of the Cross there is not only offering but destruction: the destruction of the humanity. The offering, as in the Old Testament, is one of destruction as well as a gift to God. In the Eucharist the risen Christ continues that sacrifice by choosing to be present in his glorified humanity, under signs of separation, the bread broken, the wine poured out. We as Christians are called participators, as it were, in that sacrificial adoration, through what St Paul says in Galatians 2.20: 'it is not I but Christ living in me'. How does that theme of destruction, that theme of annihilation, as the French writers put it, combine with a theology of the glorified resurrection of the humanity of Christ? Is that a profitable way of looking at sacrifice and in particular Eucharistic sacrifice and, therefore, at the way in which Christ exercises his priesthood in the Church today?

The Archbishop:

That is a matter which was the subject of a great deal of discussion in the twentieth-century Catholic theology of the Eucharistic sacrifice, and I suppose that some theologians would put a largish question mark against giving quite so much stress to the destruction, the annihilation side of it.

That sacrifice in the conditions of a sinful world involves separation, cost and death is a fact about the sinful world. You might say that in an unfallen world there would only be the sacrifice of thanksgiving, so to speak. There would only be the lifting up of a grateful gift to God and the cost and the joy would be inseparable. In a world where rebellious human wills have constantly frustrated that purpose, the one who gives himself to God is one who risks precisely what we see in the Cross and, whatever you make of this language, precisely paying the price of sin is what has to be talked about there. So certainly in the Eucharist we commemorate and bring ourselves into the presence of, or make present, however you want exactly to phrase that, a reality which is a death and a breaking.

The truth of that very deep-rooted French devotional habit of thought is that there is no Mass without breakage and I have often reflected on the immense significance of the words in the Western liturgy and the Book of Common Prayer introducing the institution narrative, 'in the [same] night in which he was betrayed', which I find again and again, as I say it at the altar, remind me that this is the night in which he was betrayed. The moment in which I am now celebrating is the night in which he was betrayed, and I am the Judas at the table too. And that has to be there in the Eucharist: the sense of a brokenness which is involved in precisely the sin that is being mended in the offering. Somehow it is a double vision, a shot-silk kind of vision, that we have in the Eucharist, which no one devotional habit or set of images can finally get right. What is happening in the Eucharist is the breaking, the tearing apart of the incarnate one by sin; because it is the sovereign divine will and perfect human will in perfect combination which is making that happen then the reality which is there in the Eucharist is not

17

simply the death, it is the whole self-offering of the Son to the Father. That comes across wonderfully in Gregory Dix in some of the most central and memorable pages of *The Shape of the Liturgy*. What we are saying about the Eucharist is exactly what you would have to say about the Fourth Gospel. There is no way of speaking about the breaking and the bloodshed that is not also talking about the glory. There is no talking about the eternal glory that is not talking about the breaking and the bloodshed. So, with some caution about underlining too heavily the word 'destruction' there, the instinct that says, 'Yes, the Mass is about the Cross', is a truthful one. You then have to ask, 'And what is the Cross about?', and you go to another level of theological reflection.

The Revd Dr Martin Warner:

I was struck by what you said about worship and mission and also in the earlier part of your talk about Moses gathering human beings into a people. Reflecting on the whole business of what we are as the Church and how we offer worship, and mindful of how Nicholas Lash has written about that recently, about the universal vocation of the Church to be the gathering of the whole human race before God – I wonder whether you could say something about how we might map out our relations to people of other faiths in this universality.

The Archbishop:

God makes worship possible: that is axiomatic. True worship is worship in spirit and truth; God's action is at the root of worship. We have been given the gift and the grace, we believe, as Christians to enter consciously, freely and fully into that. We have the words that express this reality, we have the means of communicating it, we have the effective sacramental signs. I would not want to relativize any of that while, at the same time, feeling perfectly free to recognize that by God's gift and grace worship does happen in other environments.

One of the challenges of the interfaith encounter is always to look and listen as carefully as we can for what in the worship of another religious tradition carries the marks of the Christlike action that we live in the Church. I do not much like the text-book polarities of pluralism and inclusivism and exclusivism. I do not think it is as neat as that: they all have their problems. But if I had to locate myself on that map, I would go for some sort of inclusiveness theory that allowed me to say Christ is supremely freely active in the Church but the very fact that Christ is supremely freely active in the Church does not confine his freedom to act, even unrecognized, in many other situations. I am not at all an advocate of what is usually called interfaith worship. I will happily sit in silence with a Buddhist or a Muslim; but I will not know quite what I am doing if I try to phrase a prayer with them, because I know I have to say, at some point, 'through Jesus Christ our Lord'. It is not just as a sort of gesture, or a nodding of the head, but because I cannot begin to think about prayer without that. I do not see what we are doing if we are not doing that. And if that is what we are doing, in the immortal words of Gilbert and Sullivan, 'why not say so?'

We need discrimination and common sense, patience, listening and charity, a ready assumption that if Christ truly is free then Christ's freedom may pop up all over the place, then that is wonderful. We have this wonderful theological core of all our belief that what is real, distinctive and essential about Christ is that Christ is the centre, the animating centre of the whole of the new humanity. That means where new humanity begins to come to life in ways that are manifestly Christlike, we can say Christ is at work. We know that and we can affirm that because of where we stand in Christ. In my limited experience of inter-faith encounter, the odd thing is that people in other traditions do not mind you saying that. On the whole people prefer to know where they are with Christians. The rather strange idea that it is somehow discriminatory or elitist or arrogant to affirm where you stand – in the realities on the ground of interfaith encounter, it is not so.

I have been involved, in the last couple of years particularly, in dialogue with Muslims, and that has been very instructive.

The whole notion that that is a dialogue which ought to be conducted with mutual respect means precisely to me that in respecting my dialogue partner I also respect my own commitment and expect them to do the same. I do not assume that I can only express respect or win respect by saying, 'Well, I am not really sure about where I am coming from'; I think that is nonsense. The real learning experience, the real expansion of mind and spirit that comes in dialogue, is when we do know where we are coming from and at times there is this rather wonderful, miraculous sense of 'Goodness, that really rings a bell. Yes, I see what you mean, yes. And what we would say is . . .' and then the discussion unfolds and can be very, very exciting.

Likewise, in the less formal but regular contacts I have had over the years with Buddhists, I come back again and again to thinking, 'Yes, that is so illuminating', and the Buddhist knows many things that I do not know. But I know some things the Buddhist does not know and I am not going to pretend about that. I love sitting in quiet with Buddhist friends on certain occasions; the quiet is a gift, a reality shared between us for which I am deeply grateful. And I understand it as my being in Christ and being offered by Christ to the Father. The Buddhist will say something different. But unless we share something of the discipline of sitting together we are not going to be able to talk at all.

So, it is a varied picture, but I do not think we ought either to be bullied into relativism on this, (and there is plenty in and out of the Church which does bully us into relativism) or for that matter be bullied into a kind of exclusivism which closes its eyes deliberately and unimaginatively to the gifts that can be received when there is really respectful dialogue.

An image that I have sometimes used for this is, if you like nineteenth-century English fiction, it is possible to read and enjoy both Dickens and Trollope, let us say. You might want to say, as I would want to say, that Dickens is the greater author. Dickens's world is a bigger, truer one than Trollope's. If I were asked which reveals depths that I need to encounter that are transforming, it is Dickens. On the other hand, there are some things that Trollope knows a lot more about than Dickens and perhaps, in a fully responsive, flexible, truthful conducting of my life in the world, Dickens may be the shaping force of it all, but I need to know what Trollope knows, I need to learn a bit there as well. And that is often what I feel when I am talking to Buddhists. I know what I believe about the objectivity of God, the creation of the world, the nature of prayer. Buddhists know some things about the disciplines of silence, some things about the understanding and education of selfish desire, that ring enough bells in my Christian world for me to say, 'I need to learn, I need to listen. I need to hear what they know as well.'

The Revd Jonathan Baker:

As a conference largely of ordained priests, and bearing in mind that the Eucharist re-presents the self-offering of the Son to the Father, what is it that we offer as priests of the New Covenant, and, specifically, what is it that we bring to the celebration of the Mass?

The Archbishop:

The ordained priest in the Church is there so that the community becomes actively and self-consciously the Church Catholic, the Body. Without a ministry in the Church continuous and recognizable, the way we believe the ordained priesthood is, there would always be that risk of communities defining themselves and turning in on themselves. Part of the ministry of the ordained priesthood is, therefore, maintaining what I am tempted sometimes to call the flow of Christ's blood in the body. That is the real recognizability and connectedness of community to community, so that the prayers of Christians become the prayer of the Church.

The ordained priesthood is there not only to tell the Church that it is the community of the baptized, but to activate the reality of the Church as the community of the baptized. Therefore, the priest's relationship with the quality, the character of what it is to be baptized is central. It is not to say simply the priest is just a special case of a baptized person – it would have to say a bit more than that – but that the priest's role is closely bound up with that recognition of the essence of what it is to be baptized. It is to do with making Christ and the community contemporary, and the night in which he was betrayed is now. Maundy Thursday, Good Friday, Easter Sunday and the end of all things is now in the Eucharist. The most significant thing we can, in our self-understanding as ordained priests, glean from this is that sense of the liberation of being rooted in the eternal priestly activity of Christ, of being endowed with the freedom to summon, activate and articulate the prayer of the baptized; not to speak our own words here but the words of the Body.

I do not think that we can really grow up as priests unless and until we have some sense of how, in that context, justification by faith works. Like Luther throwing his inkwell at the devil, we likewise are in a good position to throw inkwells, or modern equivalents, at the devil. I do not have to 'make it up' as a priest and in one utterly bizarre way we have it so easy as priests. We are in the one place where the words of Christ's body are given to us to speak, and the acts of Christ's body are given to us to perform. At the end of the day that is all we have to do. The rather odd thing is, of course, that wonderful doing-nothing-but-Christ which is the essence of priesthood is so very difficult because we would love to justify ourselves in all sorts of other ways: by being charismatic leaders, brilliant teachers, successful archbishops. That is not it. But if we can hear that Good News, which is the heart of our own priesthood and spirituality, there is much to be grateful for.

Notes

1 Thomas Aquinas, *Summa Theologiae*, III, 22.
2 See Augustine, Sermons 227, 229, 229a and esp. 272.
3 J. B. Torrance, *Worship, Community and the Triune God of Love* (Downers Grove, 1996), p. 20.
4 David Jenkins, *Free to Believe* (London, 1991), p. 77.

2

All for Jesus

Keith Newton

And when I am lifted from the earth I shall draw all men to myself.

(John 12.32)

What a great privilege it is to preach at this Synod on the one hundred and fiftieth anniversary of the foundation of our Society. However, I have also been wondering what Fr Lowder and the other five priests who met in 1855 in the House of Charity would make of a bishop preaching at a Synod, let alone the fact that there are so many Brethren here in episcopal orders. Bishops, after all, often gave them a difficult time. I suspect some of them might have agreed with the Revd Sydney Smith when he said: 'I must believe in Apostolic Succession, there being no other way to account for the descent of the Bishop of Exeter from Judas Iscariot.' Though, I hasten to add, for the benefit of those from that diocese, that Sydney Smith died in 1845, so no disrespect to the present bishop is intended.

Those priests and others like them were called 'ritualists' though it would be a mistake to think they were only interested in the outward trappings of the Catholic faith. Far from it; those things were simply the signs and symbols of a profound belief in the Incarnation and the continuing presence of Christ in his Church and in the sacraments he gave us. They put into practice in their parishes that belief put so succinctly by St Leo the

23

Great: since our Lord is no longer visible among us everything that was visible has passed into the sacraments.[1]

One hundred and fifty years later so much of what they were reviled and persecuted for has become common practice in the Anglican Communion. Candles, incense, vestments, holy water; all these things are in common usage and very few turn a hair. You can even obtain a faculty for a tabernacle in some dioceses and the Archbishop of Canterbury has been seen giving Benediction.

However, we should not fool ourselves. There are many similarities between the Victorian world and that of the early part of the twenty-first century. The Catholic faith is being undermined and is under attack in our church. Clergy, whilst not put into jail, are discriminated against for holding on to Catholic truth; the sacraments of marriage and orders are particularly threatened. We live in a world where private opinions have taken the place of revealed truth. I briefly mention these things to remind us that what those six priests faced in 1855 is not totally dissimilar from what some of us face today.

I think it was the late Archbishop Michael Ramsey who made a comment that preaching was about reminding people of what they already know, and that is simply what I intend to do this afternoon; to remind you what this Society stands for and what you and I as Brothers are committed to.

In 1856 Fr Lowder wrote:

> It was so ordered also, by God's good providence, that a society of priests had lately been founded in London, called the Society of the Holy Cross. Its objects are to defend and strengthen the spiritual lives of the clergy, to defend the faith of the Church, and to carry on and aid mission work both at home and abroad.[2]

Three things: personal holiness, a proclamation of the faith as we have received it, and zeal for evangelism and mission. The circumstances may have changed but our core values have not and we would all do well to recommit ourselves as priests to the spirituality of the Cross, which must be about a life of sacrifice.

I have also been pondering those famous words of a former Master, Fr Mackonochie, that the Brethren of the Society must 'dig a pit for the Cross'. I am sure many of you, like me, have visited the traditional site of Calvary and touched the place where it is said the Cross was positioned so that Jesus could be lifted from the Earth. Digging a pit for the Cross must be about preparing the ground so that Jesus may be raised up. 'And when I am lifted from the earth I shall draw all men to myself.' Raised in our lives, raised in the Church, and raised in the world.

Lifting up Jesus through the holiness of our lives. Both the reading from the Acts and the Gospel from Luke speak of our role, with all the baptized, to be witnesses to Christ's resurrection and we must witness not only with our words but with our lives.[3]

Of course, the statutes of our Society require us to take our prayer life seriously but there is more to it than that; we must have lives of integrity. What we say, what we preach, and how we live must speak eloquently of Christ if we are to raise him high. There can be no such thing as a private life for a priest, as though we can separate our priestly vocation from who we are at other times. This means our relationships with our families and our friends and our moral standards are just as important as our pattern of prayer and celebration of the sacraments.

I remember a story told of an African priest's wife who listened to her husband preaching every Sunday until she could bear it no longer. She left the church one Sunday, returned home and packed all the furniture onto the parish van and drove it back to the church where the service was continuing. He watched amazed as his wife moved the furniture into the church piece by piece until he could bear it no longer. 'Wife, what are you doing with our furniture?' he cried. She replied, 'I thought from now on we would live in here as you are a much nicer person in church.'

We have been privileged to have witnessed in the last few weeks a powerful expression of the integrity of the priesthood in the life and even more the death of Pope John Paul II as he united his suffering with the Passion of the Saviour and followed the way of the Cross.

Preaching at a Society Synod in 1873 Fr Bennett, the Vicar of Frome, said:

> Our preaching, our eloquence, our talents, our writing, our books, our pamphlets, our churches, our altars, our own very souls' spiritual condition, must be stripped and laid bare, so that we may lie down on that cross and be nailed to it, and be lifted up as a spectacle to the world, naked of everything as Jesus was.[4]

Those words reflect perfectly the holy death of the Holy Father and should be an inspiration to us all as we imperfectly try to live out the discipline of the crucified Saviour in every aspect of our own lives.

We must be fearless in proclaiming the true faith so that Jesus may be raised up and glorified in his Church. I was quite surprised the other day when a member of a congregation thanked me for using the Holy Name of Jesus in my sermon. A priest in one diocese I know has a book open for betting on when the diocesan will mention Jesus in a sermon. Now these may seem to be little things but I suspect they are symptomatic of a really serious problem: a lack of trust in the words of Jesus in Scripture being authoritative for our doctrine and our ethics. In my opinion the issue of the ordination of women to the priesthood and episcopate is merely a symptom of a much deeper problem. The question is: has God acted and revealed himself in Jesus, a revelation which challenges us about the way we conduct our lives, or is our religion little more than a way of expressing our deepest human aspirations, where what I feel becomes the guiding principle of my life and more significant than revealed truth, and where personal opinion is confused with faith? Saint Paul warned how the wise of the world would think us foolish for preaching Christ crucified.

I am delighted that in this anniversary we have put Jesus at the centre where he ought to be; our conference is about Christology and our great celebration is about standing up for Jesus together. But here lies our problem: too often we do not stand together either for common support or with a common vision. The coming years are going to be difficult for us all but if we are to remain Catholic Anglicans we need to forge an ecclesiology which is robust and coherent and ensure the Church makes that possible. We cannot simply keep drawing lines in the sand and standing behind them.

Finally, we are to have zeal for mission so that Christ is lifted up in the world. In today's Gospel the disciples are told that the message is to be preached to all the nations beginning from Jerusalem. It was a movement from the confines of Judaism, which they understood, into the hostile Gentile world and it was nothing less than the continuing of Christ's mission: 'Father, as you sent me into the world I have sent them into the world' (John 17.18).

He stirs us to grasp a new and lively understanding of our particular sharing in his mission. He sends us forth to be bearers of the Good News, sharing in the divine mission which was his from the Father. Mission is the task of the Church and we, as members of this Society, must be committed to it. We were not called to be priests, we did not become members of this Society, in order to be chaplains to congregations but to be fellow missionaries with Christ under the sign of his Cross.

Who knows where we will be led in the future but for the present we have a vocation to live out. Mordecai's words to Esther can give us some encouragement: 'Who knows,' he said, 'perhaps you have come to the throne for such a time like this' (Esther 4.14). Who knows, perhaps we have been called to the priesthood to be faithful in such a time like this.

My prayer is that that at this anniversary we will commit ourselves to Fr Lowder's vision and lift up Jesus in our lives, in his Church and in the world. And we could have no better rallying call than the words of that famous hymn from John Stainer's *Crucifixion*:

All for Jesus! All for Jesus,
This our song shall ever be;
For we have no hope nor saviour
If we have not hope in thee.

'And when I am lifted from the earth I shall draw all men to myself.'

27

Notes

1 See Pope Leo the Great, Sermon 2 *On the Ascension*, appointed for the Office of Readings in the Divine Office, Friday after Ascension.
2 C. F. Lowder, *Twenty One Years in St George's Mission* (London, 1877), pp. 16–17.
3 Acts 13:26–34; 1 Corinthians 18–25 [read but not referred to]; Luke 24:35–48.
4. ACTA Proceedings of the Society 1873, Pusey House Library Papers.

3

The Architecture of the Priesthood

Barry Swain

[Ye] are built upon the foundation of the apostles and prophets,
Jesus Christ himself being the chief corner stone; In whom all
the building fitly framed together groweth unto an holy temple
in the Lord: In whom ye also are builded together for an habita-
tion of God through the Spirit.

(Eph. 2.20–22)

1. Building a bridge

How often we have all heard this brief gobbet of St Paul's Epistle
to the Ephesians. It is part of his stirring exhortation to them, and
because, of course, God is servant neither to time nor space, it is
an exhortation to us just as well. How often, though, have we
ever thought of its architectural metaphor? At times, Anglicans
and, yes, even Anglican Catholics can be too involved in their
buildings. Even in the United States, on the East Coast, church
buildings can be up to three hundred and fifty years old, though
most are Victorian. Often in churches in Britain and the USA,
we find on tables at the rear of the church no devotional mater-
ials, nothing explaining the faith or any aspect of it, but we do
find a pamphlet about the building. In a religion which is strongly incarnational, like Catholic Christianity, this is perhaps no

surprise. We incarnate, as it were, the Church, the mystical Body of Christ, in a building. There are both positive and negative aspects of this preoccupation, but that is not our concern today.

I wonder instead if you would consider for a moment the metaphor of the Architecture of the Priesthood. As with any building, the foundation was laid long before the act of building began. God laid this foundation, and decided on the spot where the building should be erected, that is on the man in whom he lay the foundation. We had to attend to the foundation, realize and understand what the Master Builder has intended it for, and respond to that overture of His. In due course, building began: we began to have inner stirrings about our vocation, we spoke to our priest, we went off, likely as not, to a selection conference, we spoke to a bishop, and eventually we went, God help us, to a theological college. These were the final preparations of the foundation and the ground floor. At the moment of ordination, as the Chrism dried to a fragrant and slightly greasy residue, the work of foundation building was over. Now the real building was to begin. But what kind of structure?

In the Epistle to the Hebrews it is written:

> But Christ being come an high priest of good things to come, by a greater and more perfect tabernacle, not made with hands, that is to say, not of this building; . . . And for this cause he is the mediator of the new testament, that by means of death, for the redemption of the transgressions that were under the first testament, they which are called might receive the promise of eternal inheritance. (Heb. 9.11, 15)

Here again we think of the builder, erecting a spiritual building, which will serve as a great temple, not made with hands but erected with grace, prayer, willingness to embrace vocation. 'And for this cause', he says, 'he is the mediator of the new testament.'

We are all well accustomed to thinking of Our Lord as the mediator of the New Testament, the New Jerusalem, between God the Father and man. Our Lord, both entirely divine and entirely human, is in fact the perfect Mediator. But as priests we know that we also share in his vocation in all its aspects, not just imitating him, albeit unworthily, in saying Mass, in offering absolution, in healing, in preaching, and above all in acts of love, but also in his vocation as mediator. But what does it mean to say we are mediators?

The Protestant Reformers thought it meant that the priest got in the way of people in their relationship with God. They drew the mistaken inference that if a mediator exists, then one cannot also approach the other party directly. Such a conclusion is clearly false. To say that Our Lady can be asked to pray to Our Lord on our behalf does not in any sense imply that such inter- cession is required, only that it is possible and available, salutary and efficacious.

A mediator is one who comes between. Saint Paul, writing to the foolish and bewitched Galatians, reminds them that 'a medi- ator is not a mediator of one' (Gal. 3.20): there must be two parties between whom the mediator exists. The important thing to remember, though, is that the mediator can be fulfilling his vocation to be 'between' two parties or two persons for one of two reasons. He can be, as in United Nations parlance, a medi- ator between two parties in order to keep them apart. The medi- ator can also fulfil his vocation to be a mediator between two in order to bring them together.

In architectural terms, we can make this distinction even clearer. There are two ways for a priest to mediate between God and man, either as a wall or as a bridge. A wall is built, brick by brick, or stone by stone, to come between. It does its work very well if it is built well. An overrated American poet noted that 'good fences make good neighbours' but good walls and fences more often denote estrangement between parties. A wall comes between very well; it does its job as a mediator by keeping the two apart.

The other architectural project which can mediate is a bridge. We might think of some architectural marvels, like Isambard Kingdom Brunel's spectacular bridge over the Avon Gorge at Clifton in Bristol or the Brooklyn Bridge in my own city. In each of these cases, before the bridges it was entirely possible to cross the divide: one simply went by boat or went the long way round. But a bridge does not simply make a journey shorter or more convenient, it has a very powerful psychological effect: it joins the two sides so that they seem as one.

Every priest has before him the choice of what kind of mediator he will be. It is rarely the case that a priest decides to act as a wall between God and man. What more normally happens is that we are at different times of our lives and ministries walls and bridges by turns. Every opportunity missed to further God's kingdom and care for his faithful lays another brick in the wall, but every sacrament, every blessing, every prayer, every healing, every sincere effort to help, to prosper, to nurture, to edify, these all place supports in the bridge.

Each of us has the inestimable privilege and benefit of being connected to God. We have formally been connected to God as his priests, through an unbroken chain of men who have been called to serve him humbly in this special way. So far from exaltation in this calling, we must be humbled by its radical demands and our knowledge of how little honour we often do them. We have been called, as angels have not, to touch the Body of Christ. We have been called, as Our Lady and St Joseph were not, to hear confessions and give absolution. We have been called, as even Our Lord no longer does, to tend his pilgrim people here on Earth. Yes, we are in touch with the infinite, with the divine. We feel the brush of angels' wings on our shoulders. But we are also rooted in the human, in the physical world, in the life of Christ's people as they go about their daily lives. In this position, entirely because we share in Our Lord's priesthood, for we have none of our own, we are privileged to act as bridges between the seen world of London today – the City with its frenzied commerce; Fleet Street, wherever it is located now, with its fevered brow; indeed with the Queen in a very fraught week, with ordinary people in offices, with shopgirls leaving work to meet their boyfriends at an Indian takeaway, with the unemployed mother of two, with those who are sad or discouraged or oppressed or careworn, with the HIV patient in hospital, with the elderly woman alone at home and afraid to die. But whether in London, as we are today, or in New York, my own city, so similar in many ways, or in a suburban setting, or a country town, we are not only in touch with the human, the pedestrian, the quotidian. We are also in touch with the divine by virtue of who we are and who we have been called to be.

2. The dwelling-place of God

So many of your churches will have exactly the same feature as my church at home. In the midst of all the masonry, brick, mortar, stained glass, statuary, wooden pews, tile floor, and everything else that makes up church buildings as we know them, will be a small, beehive-shaped object with a silk covering over it. It is, of course, the tabernacle and it is the only reason to justify a church building at all. The purpose of any church is not to provide a place for people to pray, not to allow them to meet to have jumble sales, coffee mornings or bring-and-buys. It is not to serve the community. It is not to evangelize the world and bring Christ to its attention. It is not even to have a place in which to say Mass. It can and does do all these things, and that is fine, but they can all be done without a church building, and were for the first few hundred years of the Church, except I am not sure they had jumble sales in pre-Constantinian times. No, the purpose of this beautiful building is to keep the Blessed Sacrament safe, dry, available and worshipped. In this way, God is with us, Emmanuel. But has it ever occurred to you how odd it is that the House of Bread, the Bethlehem, that he dwells in, is so temporary, so impermanent?

Some years ago, when I was Rector of St Clement's, Philadelphia, the church of one of our other Catholic parishes in the city burnt to the ground. The rector, doing what any of us would do, tried to remove the Blessed Sacrament, but found the way to the key was barred. With two helpers he picked up and carried out the one thing absolutely necessary to save, the whole tabernacle itself. When they emerged from the smoking building carrying this object with its precious Contents, I was just arriving, having received his first phone call. It occurred to me very powerfully that he had one of two choices: either to look at the burnt church and think 'Ichabod . . . the glory of the Lord has departed the temple' (1 Sam. 4.21), or to look at what he held in his hands and say, 'Alleluia! God is with us!'

If you recall, by the end of the book of Exodus, Moses and the children of the Hebrews had been through an enormous ordeal. They had been in bondage in Egypt, had been through the plagues and Pharaoh's capricious change of mind, and then the anguish of the first Passover and the flight from Pharaoh and his host. God had saved them at the Red Sea, but there were many more harrowing ordeals to follow. Finally, God gave them the Ten Commandments and, so far from thanking God for his blessings, they erected and worshipped the golden calf. How simple and familiar to us is Aaron's answer to Moses: 'Well, I just put the gold in the furnace, as you do, and out came this calf.' Not really my responsibility at all. It is then that God orders the fashioning of the tabernacle as his dwelling-place with his pilgrim people. Although the specifications of the tabernacle are elaborate, the structure is not. It is made to be on the move, to be present with his people. It is not a fixed building but a tent. God would dwell with them, move with them, be almost as one of them, dwelling, as they did, in a tent. And when they went to the tent, there they found him: 'And Moses took the tabernacle, and pitched it without the camp, afar off from the camp, and called it the Tabernacle of the congregation. And it came to pass, that every one which sought the LORD went out unto the tabernacle of the congregation, which was without the camp' (Exod. 33.7).

Eventually, the Temple at Jerusalem replaced the tabernacle, but from the very beginning of his experience with his people fleeing bondage, God dwelt with them in a tent. What does this mean?

The first and most obvious conclusion is that this is an important fact about God which he wished to share with his people. The Egyptians built huge temples to their gods and to their own memory; indeed the Hebrews had been occupied in rearing these structures. Ra, Thoth, Anubis and all the rest had permanent and impressive temples. The Hebrews' God lived in a tent which they themselves had to carry. Here we are being taught the same fact as in the Epistle to the Hebrews, 'For here have we no continuing city, but we seek one to come' (Heb. 13.14). God himself moves about, dwells in a tent with his people, and this teaches us that we ourselves are not to regard this life, this world, as our permanent home, but as a place of sojourning, living in tents, until we reach the Promised Land. When the Hebrews forgot that fact, they got into trouble; just ask the prophets. When we forget that fact, we get into trouble too.

It is a salient and important fact for priests to remember too. We often act and talk as if we are embedded in our current cir- cumstances. If we are in a place long enough, we often come to feel as though we own the church and that in a deep sense we belong there. Such is far from the truth. We are there only because God has asked us to be for a time. As stewards, we own nothing, we simply look after what we have been entrusted with until the term of stewardship is ended. Most of us have had the experience of moving on from a church. I have now left two churches, one after a time as curate, another after a time as curate and then incumbent, to move on at the prompting of the Holy Spirit. It is not easy. All we have known and loved, and even the less attractive aspects in a place, are familiar and we are loath to leave them. But as God journeyed with his people and sojourned with them, so must we. 'Here we have no continuing city, but we seek one to come.'

God living in a tent among his people is also a metaphor about this life. Everything in our minds, spirits, hearts and society sug- gests to us that this life, the life that we see, is what matters. Our senses rely on this to serve us. The merest suggestion that there is an unseen reality unsettles a great many people, and yet it is to this Unseen Kingdom that God asks us to point. Not only are we to live halfway there, but we are to try to influence others to do the same. 'Panta rhei, ouden menei', 'All things change, nothing remains', Heraclitus the philosopher said,[1] and it should be the priest's and the Christian's passionate belief too. Nothing in this world remains, all changes, and all this moves one inex- orably to the unseen but great realities of life. We inhabit this world for a time but our true native land is elsewhere.

We have seen extraordinary scenes of millions of people from across Europe and the rest of the globe making pilgrimage to Rome to look on the face of the Holy Father in death. I think I am correct in saying that the Holy Father travelled more miles, exerted more effort and visited more people in the service of Our Lord, his Church and the gospel than anyone else in Christian history. We became so used to him alighting from an aeroplane and kissing the tarmac in some distant land that it seemed normal, but it was not normal at all, was it? It was quite extraordinary. He, almost literally, lived in temporary housing through the whole of his pontificate and never ceased to be on the move among all peoples in the name of Christ. Has there been in our times any example of someone who, though living and ministering in this world, set his sight so much on the next?

How many of you have had this experience? You vest to say Mass on a weekday, you ring a bell, and out you go. Only one or two of the faithful have joined you. This tiny group can barely be heard making responses to the Mass. You think of all those in your church on Sundays, and indeed all those who live round about who could be there, and frustration sets in. Where are they? How can I reach them? Why are they not here?

And yet this is to lose the point. You have brought both yourself and your small band of worshippers in contact with the Unseen Kingdom of Eternity. You have approached the throne of the heavenly grace and pleaded the Sacrifice instituted by Our Lord himself. Time and space melted away and you were one with the Eternal High Priest. Countless angels bowed and adored when you said, 'This is My Body.' You held the Body of Christ in your hands as did Our Lady and St Joseph in Bethlehem. You looked on his face in his Temple as did Simeon and the prophetess Anna. You heard his words in scripture as did those who walked with him so long ago in Palestine. You fed his people as he fed the five thousand. His disciples gathered together for a meal as they did in the Upper Room. The Priest of Love made himself the victim of his own Sacrifice as he did on Calvary. He showed himself pure, spotless, white and living, as he did to Mary Magdalene in the garden. He blessed his people as he did at the

Ascension, and the Holy Spirit descended on them as surely as he did in the Cenacle on Pentecost. That is what happened, and it all happened because God lives in a tent among us. It all happened because God chose to pitch his tent with mankind, to partake of humanity, to associate us with him in his eternal priesthood, and to journey with his pilgrim people as they make their way home to him. Why should we be frustrated? We should be elated.

I wrote these talks just before Easter. Since then, Our Holy Father the Pope has died. It is quite frankly impossible for me to read these words to you this morning without thinking very deeply about the living example he has given us of the way in which a priest can be a bridge: a bridge between Catholics; a bridge between Christians; a bridge to members of other faiths; above all, a bridge between God and man. One of the most ancient titles of the Pope is 'pontifex maximus', master bridge-builder. Perhaps more than anyone in modern times, the Holy Father was faithful to that vocation and is a shining light to us in ours.

The priest lies down, as does the bridge, and offers himself as a connection between the two worlds. As we live in both, we touch both. We bring to God the human world round us for his love and care, and we bring to the world round us the world of God, their own true home, if they but knew it.

Two of my grandparents were British subjects, one a Canadian, one an American. If only I had an Australian antecedent, I would have most of you covered. But the passports that matter to us are the heavenly passports we received at baptism. Those passports have under Nationality the single word, Heaven. The priest, the mediator, has as his vocation trying to bring the holders of those passports home by stretching himself physically, mentally and spiritually between the two worlds.

Note

1 *Editors*: Not in any of Heraclitus' authentic writings, though commonly attributed to him.

4

Consecration, Coherence, Catholicity

Andrew Burnham

> You did not see Christ, but you love him; and now you believe
> in him without seeing him, and you rejoice with an inexpress-
> ible, glorious joy, as you obtain the end [to which] your faith [is
> directed], the salvation of your souls.
>
> (1 Pet. 1.8–9)

In these words, in the fresh translation of the Oxford Jesuit,
Fr Nicholas King,[1] we come close to the original readership of
the first letter of Peter: a group of second-generation Christians
in Asia Minor, 'distressed by various trials', who had to rely on
other people's first-hand stories about Jesus Christ. The Easter
faith had become a traditional faith, one that is 'handed on'.

If the faith was to endure, it could no longer depend on direct
experience of the risen Christ. The Lord had prevented the one
who felt she needed to cling to him, Mary Magdalen, from
touching him: and, though he was content to meet the need of
the natural loner, Thomas, to touch his wounds, he had warned
him, 'Because you have seen me, you have come to faith. Happy
are those who did not see and believed'.[2] Indeed, 'Happy are
those who did not see and believed' is very similar to 'You did
not see Christ, but you love him; and now you believe in him
without seeing him.'

As the Easter faith was handed on, it became more clearly a Eucharistic faith. The Orthodox theologian. Fr Alexander Schmemann, reminded us that, up to and including the time of St Basil the Great, Sunday was often called 'the eighth day'.[3] There are hints of this in today's Gospel when we learn that the risen Christ appears after 'eight days'.[4] Eight is the number of eternity: God creates the world in six days, rests on the seventh, and inaugurates eternal life, the 'eighth day', through the resurrection of Jesus Christ from the dead. Over fifty years ago Fr Daniélou collected the numerous patristic references to the 'eighth day',[5] and Christian tradition tells us that the Eucharist and the Lord's Day were as one.

I am rehearsing these foundational facts as a reminder that we, as Catholics, do not start with a basic Christianity, upon which we build our own theological constructs. The teaching of Christianity as a series of, on the whole, historical facts, whose accuracy, however, is less important than the ethical code which ought to underlie decent behaviour, has done little in this country to keep the forces of secularization at bay.

As Catholic Christians, we start instead with the urgent reality of the Easter faith, experienced through the event of baptism and the deepening encounter day by day with the risen Christ in the Holy Eucharist. It is a tradition, preserved and handed on through the sacramental life of the Church, the Body of Christ in the world. Where Christianity has a moral and ethical message it springs from lives spent studying God's Word, lives made holy by devout participation in the sacramental life.

It follows that, for us, nothing is more important than safeguarding what might be called the principle of 'sacramental certainty'. Though God is not bound by our rules, it is truly for us a first-order issue that the sacramental life of the Church be properly ordered and properly defended. We refrain from Eucharists not rooted in the historic episcopate, not because of any lack of respect for other Christians, whose lives and worship are undoubtedly grace-filled, but because we look to 'all who hold and teach the Catholic Faith that comes to us from the apostles'.[6] In the Sacrament of the Altar, the sacrament of God's Eternal Present, we do not 'see Christ, but [we] love him; and . . . [we] believe in him without seeing him, and [we] rejoice with an inexpressible, glorious joy, as [we] obtain the end [to which our] faith [is directed], the salvation of [our] souls'.

But we must not be stiff-necked with our fellow Anglicans who see things so very differently, or indeed with our ecumenical brothers and sisters. We pray and hope that God will bless all that is done in his name: and that applies to our attitude to those whose understanding of the faith is so very different from our own. In a fragmentary world there will be Christians who will want women bishops, gay marriage, a rewrite of the Bible, a syncretistic faith, a goddess or an impersonal life-force: you name it. None of our energies should be dissipated in fighting all that. Heresy and schism, Gnosticism and heterodoxy have always been with us and many faithful Christians have flourished in error. If you doubt that, you have never met a very holy heretic, a Jehovah's Witness, for example; I have met several, and some holy liberals too. I have to say that some of the sentiments expressed on the Internet in the supposed defence of orthodoxy fill me with dismay. 'And now abideth faith, hope, and charity, these three: but the greatest of these is charity' (1 Cor. 13.13) Whatever happened to charity?

As priests of the Society of the Holy Cross, we must instead be joyful custodians of the tradition of the Easter faith, as the second and subsequent generations of Catholic Christians have received it: more guardians of the flame than wielders of the sword. We are custodians of what we are learning to call 'the beauty of orthodoxy'. Nothing is more important than our stewardship of the priesthood and the sacraments, of God's revelation of himself as our Father, of the reality of the Sacrifice of the Son of Man on the Cross and the dynamic efficacy of the Sacrifice of the Mass. As a Roman Catholic systematic theologian, Fr David Power, has put it:

> The main point . . . is that the Mass celebrated by a duly ordained priest, under whatever circumstances, is beneficial for those for

whom it is offered . . . if . . . not . . . the whole belief in the Mass, and the whole practice of the Mass, would fall apart.[7]

If there is one thing that members of the Society of the Holy Cross share, and have always shared, it is probably faithfulness to the Catholic understanding of Eucharistic faith and practice. Whether our ecclesiology has been Cyprianic, like some of yours, or papalist, like mine, we have believed that the Church of England, these last five hundred years, has been called upon to recover and continue faithful to the Eucharistic faith of the previous fifteen hundred years. Overseas bishops and clergy have variously exported and imported, been nurtured and nurtured others, in this Eucharistic faith, this Easter faith.

I want to finish by briefly setting an agenda for the Society of the Holy Cross for the months and years ahead. It harmonizes well with this Year of the Eucharist which we are celebrating. Three Cs: Consecration; Coherence; Catholicity. We must learn to consecrate ourselves once more to priestly holiness, to 'dig a pit for the Cross'. Consecration must lead us to greater coherence, as priests of the Society with a shared ecclesiology and with a shared commitment to the teaching of the Church in matters of faith and morals. In recent years and with good leadership, the Society has splendidly recovered its morale. We must now work for the kind of coherence which will insulate the boat against the ecclesiological storms that buffet us. One contribution to the coherence that is missing, I noticed at our Synod, is the absence of Africa. There are countless bishops and priests in Africa who share almost everything with us except membership of our Society. We must put that right.

Increased coherence leads us naturally to our third 'C', Catholicity. What this quite means in terms of our relationship with the ancient communion of the West, of which we are a fragment, a broken-off shard, is, as yet, no clearer than who will be the next pope.[8] Sacramental certainty would have to be part of any staying-on as Anglicans, in a way that nothing as ecclesiologically imprecise as a code of practice could provide, just as surely as our pastoral responsibility to those in our care has to be part of any ecumenical journey we will feel called, and some of us bound, to make.

I suggest we make a start on our consecration, our coherence and our Catholicity by attending more profoundly to the Eucharistic Mystery. We need the devotion of a Thomas Aquinas who, weeping with joy at the sight of the elevated host, used to say, 'Thou art the King of glory, O Christ. Thou art the everlasting Son of the Father.'[9] I have asked all the priests who look to me to come together for one of a series of days of Eucharistic Adoration in this Year of the Eucharist. Father Raniero Cantalamessa, preacher of the Pontifical Household, in a Good Friday sermon in St Peter's Basilica this year, explored the text 'Ave verum corpus'.[10] 'It is not possible', says Fr Cantalamessa, 'to find a better way to bring to light the link between the Eucharist and the Cross. Written in the thirteenth century as an accompaniment to the elevation of the Host at Mass, it serves us today equally well as our salutation of Christ raised up on the Cross.'[11]

The medievals were preoccupied by the identity of the Eucharistic Host with the natural Body of Christ, born of Mary and immolated on the Cross; and indeed we should continue to be similarly preoccupied. And yet an earlier, more Eastern, preoccupation, an emphasis that has been recovered in modern Eucharistic piety, is that of our text from 1 Peter, with which I shall finish. This preoccupation is that the One whom we encounter in the Eucharist is the Son of Man himself, 'risen, ascended, glorified', Jesus our great high priest who at the altar in heaven leads us in prayer to the Father. It is this Jesus of whom Peter or his disciple is writing when he says: 'You did not see Christ, but you love him; and now you believe in him without seeing him, and you rejoice with an inexpressible, glorious joy, as you obtain the end [to which] your faith [is directed], the salvation of your souls.'

Notes

1 *The New Testament Freshly Translated* by Nicholas King (Stowmarket, 2004).

2 John 20.29 (King's translation). The Gospel reading at Mass was John 20.19–31.

3 Alexander Schmemann, *Introduction to Liturgical Theology*, 2nd edn (London, 1966), p. 62.

4 John 20.26. There is an allusion also in 1 Pet. 3.30, where we learn that 'eight people were saved'.

5 Jean Daniélou, 'La Théologie du Dimanche', in *Le Jour du Seigneur* (Paris, 1948), pp. 120ff.

6 Roman Eucharistic Prayer 1 (ICEL).

7 David Power, *The Sacrifice We Offer* (Edinburgh: 1987), p. 128.

8 *Editors:* This talk was given on 6 April 2005; Benedict XVI was elected on 19 April.

9 John Saward, *The Beauty of Holiness and the Holiness of Beauty* (San Francisco, 1997) p. 96.

10 The homily was published at Easter ZENIT on the Internet.

11 Father Raniero Cantalamessa, 'True Body, Truly Born of the Virgin Mary', available at www.zenit.org/english/visualizza.phtml?sid=68364 (accessed 27 January 2006).

5

Anglicans, ARCIC and Ecclesiology

Christopher Hill

On Monday morning [4 April 2005] I dodged a question on the Southern Sound *Drive-in* programme asking me in relation to the funeral of Pope John Paul whether the Archbishop of Canterbury ought to go to the funeral in Rome rather than lead a certain Service of Prayer and Dedication in St George's, Windsor. I said I had no inside knowledge about these things; that it was a matter for Lambeth Palace; and until the date for the papal funeral was definitely set and invitations sent from Rome, it was a hypothetical question. I reverted to type: in other words, to the style of a Lambeth *apparatchik* giving a diplomatic answer. As the day unfolded, however, news emerged. I received a call from Ruth Gledhill, Religious Correspondent of *The Times*, who informed me, before the news broke, that the Prince of Wales had delayed his civil wedding by a day and that the Archbishop was expected to go to the funeral. She talked over with me the significance of the Archbishop going to Pope John Paul II's funeral. In spite of the alleged demise of ARCIC, in spite of Anglican uncertainty over women bishops and human sexuality, this was a major ecumenical event. I confirmed her view that it was. And we all pray for Archbishop Rowan and commend the soul of John Paul II at this time.

The Bishop of Rome sent Augustine to evangelize the English. Whether as Patriarch of the West, Universal Primate or simply as the head of the Roman Catholic Church, the Bishop of Rome deserves our respect, our prayers and our fraternal concern. As ARCIC II noted, there is already a kind of recognition of a universal primacy, a primacy of love which is more than a primacy of honour, if somewhat less than an ultramontane interpretation of the First Vatican Council. Members of the Society of the Holy Cross have been amongst the first Anglicans to recognize and articulate this. And you have been ecumenically right so to do.

What do we now say about Anglicans, ARCIC and the Pope? I want to suggest that the Roman Catholic Church and the churches of the Anglican Communion have a common, or rather related, agenda of greater significance than the presenting issues of contemporary difficulty between us.

In Pope John Paul II's encyclical *Ut Unum Sint* (1995), which we may properly take as his ecumenical testament, he repeated and emphasized the irrevocable commitment of the Roman Catholic Church to ecumenism as expressed in the Second Vatican Council. He also acknowledged that his own office was a source of difficulty between Christians, as well as a potential and actual ministry of unity. He invited a dialogue on this ministry, to which the House of Bishops of the Church of England made a substantial, eirenic and positive reply.

But there is more to say than simply that the office of the Bishop of Rome is an ecumenical problem or an ecumenical opportunity. The *raison d'être* of all episcopal ministry is to signal the unity within the local, diocesan church and between that church and other churches in the wider communion of churches. It is also to signal the unity of the local diocesan church with the apostolic church itself. To put it in shorthand, episcopacy is to signal *synchronic* and *diachronic* catholicity and apostolicity. This is the eccesiological argument of ARCIC I and II about episcopacy before we reach the question of primacy.

Such an Anglican, Roman Catholic and Orthodox, and now at least in part Lutheran and even Reformed, ecclesiology is an ecclesiology of *koinonia, communio*. Primacy, whether regional or universal, is still within and never apart from such an episcopal ministry of communion. The Pope is who he is because he is the Bishop of Rome. Even Vatican I was very careful to describe the ministry of the Bishop of Rome as *vere episcopalis*. Now we can look at how collegiality and conciliarity fit in here; ARCIC has consistently argued for a balance between primacy, collegiality, conciliarity and synodal aspects of authority.

What is the relationship between the local (that is, in this context, the diocesan) and universal church? Paul Handley, writing in *The Times* about the choices facing the Roman Catholic Church with the election of a new pope, was crystal clear that this is the issue. I believe he is right. He saw questions such as clerical celibacy, even the ordination of women and issues in sexuality, as symptomatic of the deeper question of the authority of the local church and the universal church.

In a recently published collection of ecumenical essays by Cardinal Walter Kasper[1] four out of ten of these essays touch directly on the relation of the local to the universal church. And while I am on the subject of Cardinal Kasper, it is worth recording that in Pope John Paul II's appointment of Kasper as Cardinal President of the Pontifical Council for Christian Unity, we have a real demonstration of the inability to characterize the late Pope in simplistic terms such as 'liberal' or 'conservative'. Kasper has consistently, if properly diplomatically, rebutted the centralizing ecclesiological tendency of other Vatican dicasteries by insisting that the Vatican II formula *subsistit in*, which replaced the original draft *est*, and denies a strict identity between the Roman Catholic Church and the Church of Christ, takes seriously the fact that outside the visible confines of the Roman Catholic Church there are not only individual Christians but also real ecclesial structures and genuine particular churches. He also firmly expounds the reality of the local church as affirmed in Vatican II, in which the one universal Church exists in and is formed out of the local churches. Put *Ut Unum Sint* together with the appointment of Cardinal Kasper and Archbishop Rowan's attendance at the funeral of Pope John Paul II and you have an immensely powerful commitment to the search for unity despite all the obstacles, new and old.

It will not have escaped you that Anglicans too have some little concern about the local and the universal: about where and about how decisions are made in the church. Ecumenists have been saying for about twenty-five years that Anglican issues of authority, such as the ordination of women to the presbyterate and the episcopate and now issues in human sexuality, and Roman Catholic issues of authority, such as the status of Episcopal Conferences and the central appointment of bishops or determination of liturgical questions in relation to inculturization, reflect two sides of the authority coin. We are too dispersed; Rome is too centralized. The authority statements of both ARCIC I and II say the same, though not so bluntly. Now the Windsor Report has put forward quite modest proposals for the enhancement of the primacies of the Anglican Communion.[2] It has done so on the basis of a *communio* ecclesiology, already partly articulated in ARCIC I and II. Our own disagreements as Anglicans, whether in relation to women priests or bishops or the more recent debate about sexuality, should be a spur to dialogue, not an excuse to close it down. That is one additional reason I am profoundly grateful that Archbishop Rowan is going to Rome; symbols in Rome are more powerful than words. The Archbishop of Canterbury will go to the Pope's funeral wearing the Milan ring Paul VI gave to Michael Ramsey in 1966 in Rome at the church of St Paul-without-the-Walls.

The ecumenical journey will nevertheless be a long one. For me that is no reason to give up, or to short-circuit, the pilgrimage. So what of the ecclesial house we currently inhabit? I think the first thing to say is that all ecclesial houses are made of glass. Stone-throwing in any direction is therefore strictly forbidden because highly dangerous. Way back in 1993 I addressed the SSC London Chapter at St Paul's Cathedral. I had been invited by the then Master to look at the ecclesial issues facing the Church of England in relation to the ordination of women. Though booked before the vote, the meeting was after the vote. I explored options after laying out my own conviction that that development was

right. Some of what I then wrote has application today in relation to the episcopate but that is not how I want to end. My
subject is ecclesiology in relation to ARCIC. I would argue, as I
did in 1993, that Rome and Canterbury present opposite sides of
the coin of authority. I would also argue that this is because both
ecclesial traditions have flaws, fault-lines, hairline cracks that
open up unexpectedly as pressure increases. I argued that all the
churches in our unhappy divisions have such fault-lines.

Take the Orthodox churches. Their Caesaro-papism, their
assimilation to the Byzantine Imperium, makes them weak in the
face of state tyranny. Any student of Tudor Church history must
say the same of Henry or Elizabeth's Church of England; we do
all live in glass houses. I spent a few days recently in Cornwall
staying with a retired medic who spent some time in the terrible
Romanian orphanages. The reputation of the official Orthodox
Church under Ceausescu was not good. Equally the Russian
Church, which produced so much heroism and spirituality for
the best part of a century, is now, at least in part, victim to the
xenophobia and imperialism of contemporary Russian politics.
But that does not unmake it as a church. The unworthiness of
the ministers hinders not the effect of the sacrament, as we all
know, personally.

Rome, at least since the Hildebrandine reforms at the beginning of the first millennium, has needed to protect the spiritual independence of the Church and it did so by going in
the opposite direction to the East. The Pope became, in effect,
the emperor. But as Cardinal Kasper notes, the Church is not
a monarchy, not even a constitutional monarchy. The pressure
on Rome increased with the Renaissance, as dominant nation-
state empires such as that of the Spanish-Austrian Hapsburgs
or France sought to control the papacy. The Pope became an
absolute monarch in defiance of absolute monarchs. It is not
without significance that Italy and the Papal States were being
invaded at the very moment of the First Vatican Council.

Against that background the English Reformation can be seen
in context. In spite of Henry, Elizabeth and the Carolines, the
Church of England and the Anglican Churches rediscovered

something of the conciliar tradition. But it became a synodal tradition separated from wider or universal communion because of the judicial independence established from the legacy of the Henrician Reformation when, in effect, papal monarchical jurisdiction was simply transferred from one supreme monarch to another; from an unwilling but powerless pope to a power-acquisitive king. But the Church did not cease to be the Church, whether Anglican, Orthodox or now Roman Catholic. I would also want to argue for the ecclesiality of other Christian communities, on similar grounds to Vatican II. Wherever there are elements or structures of the Church, even outside formal, wider communion, there is a real, if imperfect, church or ecclesial community.

We have to live with our fractured, fault-lined ecclesiologies. Roman Catholics in the next few weeks will be thinking of the huge problems facing their part of the Church of Jesus Christ. The day-to-day control of every, or almost every, diocese in communion with Rome is a hugely stifling burden. You do not have to be a Latin American theologian to see that the centralism which only came to its apogee in the late nineteenth century, through the telegraph and the new railway which carried mail, means that in many parts of the world the Church cannot easily respond to the culture of its context. The culture of the family, the clan, the ancestors, which makes marriage and the raising of children as successors so important for most African cultures, makes the Nigerian reaction to homosexuality (there are no homosexuals, just some married men who go with men) understandable, though not unquestionable. Precisely the same culture is completely negated by official clerical celibacy. My medic from Cornwall has worked in Botswana, in Kenya and Uganda. Many ordinary Roman Catholic priests have unofficial concubines, just as the Anglo-Saxons did before the Norman episcopate enforced celibacy. Bishops always spoil the fun. When St Augustine came to England Gregory the Great gave him wise missiological counsel: adapt what is good of the Church of Rome and the Church of Gaul and make something good for the English. I am not being anti-Roman Catholic or anti-papal.

I am saying that there are really serious ecclesiological problems in Rome as well as Canterbury. It is our ecumenical duty to search together for the ARCIC balance between the local and the universal, for the primatial and the synodal, for a proper subsidiarity which means taking decisions at the lowest appropriate level – not necessarily always at the local or national level. But in the meantime we have to live with our own ecclesiological fault-lines, not complacently but realistically, recognizing that from the beginning decisions were usually taken locally, to be later endorsed, modified or rejected in a process of reception by the wider church.

I have said that Pope John Paul II cannot be categorized over-simplistically. Let me end with a story from Robert Runcie's visit to Rome in 1989. After a lengthy but good theological and pastoral discussion and an even lengthier and even happier lunch in the papal apartments, washed down with excellent Italian wine, Pope John Paul walked to the exit of the papal palace with the Archbishop. His last words on this occasion were his hope and prayer that their 'affective' collegiality would one day become also an 'effective' collegiality. The Pope was after all a brilliant linguist; his pun was delivered in English on the spur of the departing moment.

Archbishop Rowan's presence at Pope John Paul II's requiem tomorrow at St Peter's witnesses to our common experience of affective collegiality, despite all the well-known obstacles. ARCIC and our existing 'affective' collegiality prompt us further to 'effective' collegiality, a collegiality of balance which Rome and Canterbury, in their different ways, both desperately need.

Notes

1 Walter Kasper, *That They May All Be One: The Call to Unity Today* (London, 2004).
2 The Lambeth Commission on Communion, *The Windsor Report 2004* (London, 2004).

6

Anglicans, ARCIC and Ecclesiology

Mary Tanner

Like Bishop Christopher I am very aware that we are speaking on the subject of Anglicans, ARCIC and ecclesiology on the eve of the funeral of Pope John Paul II, a Bishop of Rome for whom the unity of the Church mattered intensely and who longed to see his ministry in the service of unity shared with others; a Bishop of Rome who was daring enough to invite us to help him understand better the potential of that ministry and humble enough to ask forgiveness for the wrongs of the past; a Bishop of Rome who has shown us and the world the importance of a personal, enfleshed symbol of unity at the world level.

Our current turmoil in the Anglican Communion is no reason to give up on the ecumenical pilgrimage with the Roman Catholic Church. Indeed, our problems make that journey all the more necessary, if all the more complex and challenging. Neither the Roman Catholic Church nor the Anglican Communion has its ecclesiology right. Neither of us has right the way we live out being Church. If Rome suffers from an over-centralized model of being Church, Anglicans are, as Bishop Mark Santer once put it, 'soggy at the centre'. Bishop Christopher expressed it more diplomatically when he talked of the two sides of the one coin: 'we are too dispersed: Rome too centralized'. Anglicans and Roman Catholics thus have a common or related agenda. We need one another and we cannot afford to let the current turmoil of the Anglican Communion drive us apart.

The ARCIC Agreed Statement *The Gift of Authority*, even if it has not got everything right, sets out the problems of the Anglican Communion being too dispersed, as well as the problems of the Roman Catholic Church being too centralized.[1] Nevertheless, together with Roman Catholics, through the work of ARCIC Anglicans have glimpsed a vision of what it might be like to live out the communion of the Church in this world for God's sake and the world's sake. Each of the ARCIC Agreed Statements, from the Windsor Statement on the Eucharist[2] to the Statement on Mary,[3] contributes a piece of the jigsaw puzzle that, when put together, makes up the ecclesiological vision of ARCIC. Of course, it is an ideal vision, but do not we all need ideals to beckon us on, to move us beyond the limits and the distorted landscape that we inhabit now?

In ARCIC we are offered an ecclesiology of communion (*koinonia*), the picture of a Church living in the orbit of God's own life of love, sustained and nurtured by a communion in faith, sacramental life, ministerial communion, with the historic episcopate, and structured communion, with oversight exercised in personal, communal and collegial ways, and with authority not so dispersed that it cannot be exercised; a communion focused in, and served by, the personal ministry of the Bishop of Rome. This communion is expressed in mutual support, common service and mission, and, ARCIC insists, a shared moral life, lived out in a variety of cultural contexts which give to the whole a diversity beyond anything we have yet begun to imagine. This is the ecclesiology expressed in the reports of ARCIC, most fully so in *Church as Communion*.[4] There is much more to be said about ARCIC's ecclesiology and there are contours in the ecclesiological vision of ARCIC that require further work in order to reach anything like full agreement on an ecclesiological vision. We need more work, for example, on the proper relation of local to universal, on the specific exercise of the ministry of the Bishop of Rome, on diversity in communion, on the structures and processes of decision-making in communion, on the reconciliation of ministries, on the ordination of women, as well as issues in moral life. What is clear is that there is a huge measure of shared agreement about the sort of Church God calls us to be together in and for this world. Moreover, Anglicans have already given a measure of affirmation to this vision in the response of the 1988 Lambeth Conference to the *Final Report* of ARCIC I. The Roman Catholic Church too, after *Clarifications*, has given a significant measure of approval to the direction of ARCIC.[5]

The consequence of this is that the sharp challenge before both of our communions now is whether we are willing to receive the insights of these paper agreements into our lives; whether we are prepared to embody the agreements reached in ARCIC into the very fabric of our own life in the Anglican Communion. Equally, the challenge to Rome is whether it can embody the insights of ARCIC's ecclesiology in its own life now. Are we, either of us, prepared to let the ARCIC ecclesiology be a catalyst for renewal and development; are we prepared to change? For Anglicans a part of the challenge entails considering how we might go on developing instruments of communion, structures and processes and personal ministries at a world level, that would better serve the communion of the Church and leave us less soggy at the centre. How might we develop the Lambeth Conference and assess its authority, the Primates' Meeting, the structures of the Anglican Consultative Council, even the role of the Arch-bishop of Canterbury (without turning his ministry into a rival universal primacy), in the exercise of authority in communion, to the benefit of the local/universal dynamic of the Church's life? These are precisely the questions put sharply to us in the ARCIC agreed statement *The Gift of Authority*, and they are precisely the questions put to us, independently of ARCIC, by the Inter-Anglican Theological and Doctrinal Commission in the Virginia Report.[6] One of the great disappointments at the last Lambeth Conference was the failure of the bishops to consider and respond to the ecclesiological challenges of the Virginia Report. Had the bishops concentrated more on those challenges we might not be in the present predicament. As a consequence we are in the same state as Henry Chadwick describes the fourth-century Church being in when he says: 'It was the misfortune of the church of the fourth century that it became engrossed in a theological controversy at the same time as it was working out its institutional organization to deal with such controversies'.[7] We are engaged in a controversy over moral life, which touches the communion of the Church, when Anglicans seem to have little shared understanding of Spirit-led discernment and authoritative decision-taking in the communion of local churches. We were learning how discernment in communion can happen in the way we handled the ordination of women to the priesthood and the episcopate and we are still learning about discerning the mind of Christ for the Church in the open process of reception that continues, but we failed to learn from that process and have added the difficult subject of human sexuality.[8]

The fact is that Anglicans are not doing well in receiving the ecclesiological challenges of ARCIC into the fabric of our own lives. We are slow to develop the structures of communion and processes of discernment that would enable us to respond to new controversies in the areas of faith, order or moral life. Nor have we so far done well in receiving the theological agreements of ARCIC into changed relationships with our Roman Catholic brothers and sisters in a closer shared life of faith and mission. ARCIC, after thirty-five years, has not made the difference that it ought, or could have done, either to the renewal of our Anglican internal life or to closer communion with Rome. How to receive ARCIC's ecclesiological vision remains a challenge for us.

However, the story of the reception of the ecclesiology of ARCIC is not wholly one of failure. As we entered a new millennium the responsibility for the reception of ARCIC's vision passed properly in two episcopally ordered churches from the theologians to those with oversight in both communions. Archbishop George Carey and Cardinal Cassidy, with the Pope's blessing, called together one Roman Catholic and one Anglican bishop from fourteen countries. They came two by two and were invited to reflect in their pairs on the relationship between our two communions in their own regions. They were invited to recall the ecclesiological vision of ARCIC, brilliantly set before them by Jean Tillard, Father Tillard's last gift to us before his death some weeks later.[9] The bishops were invited to reflect on the degree of agreement in faith expressed in ARCIC and to consider how Anglicans and Roman Catholics, on the basis of those agreements, might move into a new stage of what they called 'evangelical *koinonia*, evangelical communion'. At the end of their time these bishops, including the then Bishop Walter Kasper, were amazed at how much Anglicans and Roman Catholics already share, the commonality of our liturgical life, our episcopal polities, our commitment to mission. The bishops felt at home with one another. The twenty-four bishops determined to move things on, to get reception going. 'Reception' became their new holy word. They picked up the determination of Jean Tillard, when he said:

> I firmly believe that without being totally healed, the schism dividing our two communions may be, must be shrunk, diminished . . . We cannot wait until the obstacle of women's ordination is removed, an official step is now possible and must be taken now.[10]

The bishops had taken the matter of reception into their own episcopal hands. They suggested a new commission, not of theologians but of bishops, to work at the challenge of how to receive the vision of ARCIC. The new episcopal commission was to be charged with the task of formulating a declaration which would affirm the degree of agreement reached and, on the basis of that agreement, propose what appropriate commitments should be made to live a closer life and shared mission.

Remarkably swiftly a new international commission of bishops was set up, the International Anglican–Roman Catholic Commission for Unity and Mission (IARCCUM). The Commission was well on the way to publishing a declaration which would lead the two communions to embody the insights of ARCIC in a new, closer relationship of shared life and mission. The Declaration, if ratified by both communions, would then, like the Joint Declaration on Justification with the Lutherans, be celebrated around the world and its implementation would become the responsibility of pairs of bishops in each region in an exercise of shared collegiality.

The future looked promising. Anglican–Roman Catholic relations were being given a new impetus at the beginning of a new millennium. The Declaration was near completion when the work of the episcopal commission on reception was suspended because of events surrounding the consecration of Bishop Gene Robinson, a man living in an openly gay relationship. It is significant that it was not the work of the theological commission, ARCIC, that was suspended but the work of the episcopal commission, the commission that could really make a difference to Anglican–Roman Catholic lived relations. The reaction of the Roman Catholic Church was understandable. The reaction was not in the first place to the consecration of a man living in an openly gay relationship, though that is a moral problem for the Roman Catholic Church. The reaction was, in the first instance, to the fact that what had happened in the consecration in New Hampshire flew in the face of a Resolution of the college of Anglican bishops at the Lambeth Conference, which was subsequently affirmed by the Primates' Meeting, and was contrary to the express advice of the Archbishop of Canterbury. In other words it flew in the face of all the instruments of Anglican Communion at the world level.

It was Bishop Crispian Hollis, the Roman Catholic Bishop of Portsmouth and a member of IARCCUM, who expressed things most clearly in this country when he asked: 'What sort of Church are we in conversation with?' Bishop Hollis was expressing the view that he and many other Roman Catholics believed that Anglicans and Roman Catholics had certain shared agreements about the Church, about the relation of the local church to the universal Church, about the role of collegiality and primacy in the discernment of the mind of Christ, and about the exercise of authority in the Church. These agreements had been expressed in the work of ARCIC. Now the consecration in New Hampshire seemed to call those agreements into question. What Bishop Hollis was saying to Anglicans, what the Vatican was saying in suspending the work of the high-level episcopal group, it seems, was: 'What is the point of making ecclesiological agreements if you do not live according to the principle we have jointly agreed?' These reactions focused a new ecumenical question, the question of the accountability of a church to the theological and ecclesiological agreements made. What does it mean to be a trustworthy and reliable ecumenical partner? What is mutual accountability in dialogue?

Thankfully, in spite of strained relations, that 'affective bond' of communion remained. It was evident in Archbishop Rowan's attendance at Vespers in Westminster Cathedral this week and the part he was given in the service. It will be reflected in the Archbishop's attendance at the funeral of Pope John Paul II in Rome. It was also there in the response that Cardinal Kasper made to Archbishop Rowan's request to him, following the consecration of Gene Robinson, to accompany Anglicans in their turmoil. The cardinal's response was immediate and positive for, as he wrote back to Archbishop Rowan, there is no action that can any longer be considered a unilateral action which does not have implications for us both. Our relation is too close for that. The cardinal's suggestion was that Anglicans and Roman Catholics review what had happened in the Anglican Communion in the light of the ecclesiology of ARCIC. Anglicans were invited to understand their actions in the light of ARCIC's vision of the Church.

Six theologians, three from each communion, did precisely that. They reviewed what had happened in the Anglican Communion in the context of ARCIC's ecclesiology. In the mirror of ARCIC, the actions were shown to be contrary to what ARCIC had agreed about episcopacy, collegiality, primacy and discernment in the communion of the Church. The events in New Hampshire clearly contradicted the ecclesiology of ARCIC. The group reflected that how each communion acts either gives credibility to what they have agreed in their theological dialogue or calls that agreement into question. How each acts also confirms, or denies, something about the sort of life Anglicans and Roman Catholics look to live together in the future and indicates the seriousness, or lack of seriousness, of their intention to move together in conformity with what has been agreed. The group believed that the events in New Hampshire called into question the ARCIC agreements on ecclesiology. The reflections of the group were submitted to the Lambeth Commission on Communion, the commission set up by the Archbishop of Canterbury at the request of the primates of the Anglican Communion to reflect on the events in New Hampshire and New Westminster, who submitted their findings as the Windsor Report.[11]

The promise of the Windsor Report is that it reaffirms the basic ecclesiology of ARCIC, not the way of independence, naked autonomy of the local church, 'the shibboleth of autonomy' as Archbishop Robert Runcie called it, but 'autonomy in communion', a balance between appropriate provincial autonomy and necessary interdependence.[12] It affirms the place of episcopal oversight, collegiality, and primacy and the need for discernment in the communion of the Church when a matter touches the very communion of the Church, whether the matter is of faith, order or moral life. It calls for restraint on the part of a local church when a matter touches the communion of all, while insisting on space for debate of the issue, as the mind of Christ is sought in the communion of all the local churches.

How Anglican provinces respond to the Windsor Report will show whether Anglicans agree with the ecclesiology of Windsor, with its stress on autonomy in communion and on the instruments of discernment in communion. This is not a new ecclesiology, for it builds on a long tradition of Anglican ecclesiological thinking.[13] The way provinces respond to the Windsor Report will also, implicitly, tell us something about the Anglican commitment to the ecclesiological vision of ARCIC and the intention to deepen communion with the Roman Catholic Church on the way to visible unity.

The degree of 'affective communion' that exists between Anglicans and Roman Catholics has helped Anglicans to live through the crisis in Anglican–Roman Catholic relations this time. The pressure is on Anglicans to decide whether they really are committed to the ARCIC ecclesiological vision or not. There is much at stake in the responses of the provinces to Windsor, not only for the life of the Anglican Communion but also for relations with the Roman Catholic Church.

The Society of the Holy Cross, with your inclination to a truly Catholic view of the Church, may have a special vocation to keep alive the ecclesiological vision of ARCIC, the ecclesiology of communion, to interpret it to others, and to help Anglicans receive that vision into the fabric of their own lives, moving them beyond the fractured fault-lines of our ecclesiology. The way ahead is not going to be easy for Anglicans. There is already some indication of that in the responses coming in to the Windsor Report which seem to challenge both the ecclesiology of the Windsor Report and, with that, implicitly the ecclesiology of ARCIC. But it is perhaps worth remembering what Cardinal Kasper said in his homily to the bishops at Mississauga: 'One day we may wake up and rub our eyes and be surprised at what God has already done among us.'

As we look beyond the pontificate of Pope John Paul II we need to pray that the next Bishop of Rome will understand ARCIC and its challenges, not only for Anglicans but also for the Catholic Church with its over-centralization; that a new pope will encourage a conversation to continue on the relation of local to universal; that he will allow the discussion on the ordination of women to take place, for Anglicans desperately need a conversation on women's ordination with Roman Catholic partners for the sake of the open process of reception in which they are currently engaged; and that the next Bishop of Rome will go on holding out to all of us the gift of a renewed ministry of universal primacy in the service of unity. The last days have shown the enormous possibility and potential of a personal focus of unity both for Christians and for the world at large.

Notes

1 *The Gift of Authority: Authority in the Church III*, an Agreed Statement by the Second Anglican–Roman Catholic International Commission, (London and Toronto, 1999).
2 Now part of *ARCIC I: The Final Report*; see n. 5 below.

3 *Mary: Grace and Hope in Christ*, an Agreed Statement by the Anglican–Roman Catholic International Commission (London, 2005).

4 *Church as Communion*, an Agreed Statement by the Second Anglican–Roman Catholic International Commission (London, 1991).

5 *ARCIC I: The Final Report* (1982) and *ARCIC II: Requested Clarifications on Eucharist and Ministry* (1993) are both published in Christopher Hill and Edward Yarnold (eds), *Anglicans and Roman Catholics: The Search For Unity* (London, 1994).

6 *The Virginia Report: The Report of the Inter-Anglican Theological and Doctrinal Commission*, in *The Official Report of the Lambeth Conference* (London, 1998), pp. 17–68.

7 Henry Chadwick, *The Penguin History of the Church. I: The Early Church*, revd edn (Harwordsworth: 1990), p. 133.

8 Cf. Mary Tanner, 'Women's Ordination: A Credible Model for Ecumenical Decision-Making', *Anglican and Episcopal History*, 64 (1995), pp. 429–43.

9 The papers of these meetings were published in *One in Christ*, 39:1, (Jan. 2004).

10 Jean Tillard, 'Our Goal: Full and Visible Communion', *One in Christ*, 39:1 (Jan. 2004), pp. 39–50.

11 The Lambeth Commission on Communion, *The Windsor Report 2004* (London, 2004).

12 Ibid., esp. para. 82.

13 Cf. the Resolutions of Lambeth Conferences, Reports of the Eames Commission on Women and the Episcopate, and the Virginia Report.

7

Pope John Paul II: Reflections on a Life

Christopher Hill

The live radio coverage of the announcement of Pope John Paul II's election came while I was visiting Hilary, my wife, in St Thomas's Hospital, London the day before the birth of our first son. The Italian Dean of the College of Cardinals stumbled over the new pope's Polish name, Karol Wojtyla. The pundits did not catch it and when they did, most scratched their heads, for only those on the inside knew of the Cardinal Archbishop of Cracow. Hilary said to me, 'You're a useless visitor; go and look him up and do your brief.' I needed to get back to my office at Lambeth Palace to write a briefing note on the new Pope for the Archbishop of Canterbury.

The world rejoiced in the first non-Italian Pope for centuries. Only one or two people had reservations, including the late Professor Geoffrey Lampe, who thought it was all right for the Bishop of Rome to be an Italian.

Pope John Paul's achievements have been huge. He enormously strengthened the mission emphasis of the Roman Catholic Church in the developing world by his frequent, worldwide pastoral visits. He championed the coming together of world religious leaders for prayer for world peace, a cause successive Archbishops of Canterbury have encouraged and supported.

He was genuinely committed to the unity of the Christian churches. His visit to Canterbury Cathedral on 29 May 1982 was a landmark and changed the ethos of Anglican–Roman Catholic relations in this country and worldwide. I have a photograph of the Pope and the Archbishop of Canterbury at the time, Robert Runcie, kneeling together at the Shrine of St Thomas of Canterbury. Pope John Paul II courageously recognized that his own office is a stumbling block to many Christians and he invited other Christians to be in critical dialogue with him about his office and role in the Church.

Pope John Paul II must also be credited with being a major iconic factor in the demise of Eastern European Marxism. The greatest opponent of Marxism and the Soviet Empire, whether the USSR or its satellites, was without doubt the Catholic Church in Poland. Polish Marxism crumbled first and a Polish pope was a major factor in its fall. Then Russia and Eastern Germany.

But his strength was also his weakness. Brought up in a Poland which endured first Nazi and then Communist tyranny, the Church had little time for internal debate or reflection on modern culture. Any divisions would have been weakness. John Paul II was less good at understanding the secularism of the post-modern societies of the Northern Hemisphere and consequently less helpful, ultimately, to the Church, whether the Catholic Church or other churches, in working out how the gospel can be freshly translated for radically new contexts. In the developing world too the closing down of the debate about a married priesthood has had profound effects on vocations to the priesthood. Moreover, his thought remained very much Europe-centred. What of a genuinely multicultural Church?

Pope John Paul II tried to balance the conservative and radical emphases within the Church and some Roman Catholics would think he came down too heavily on the conservative side. But the story is not all one way. From time to time his appointments could only be seen as counterbalancing the current traditionalism: for example, his appointment of Cardinal Walter Kasper, who represented the Pope at the enthronement of Rowan Williams as

Archbishop of Canterbury in January 2003, as head of the Pontifical Council for Unity.

Arguably, an Italian pope might get to grips more effectively with significant divisions in the Vatican that effectively curb either initiative or delegation to local churches. There is a huge agenda for the Roman Catholic Church in the immediate future.

At a personal level I had a huge admiration and respect for the late Pope. I met him on a number of occasions, especially during the earlier years of his pontificate, and no one who met him would wish to deny his great Christian character and human engagement with all he met. I was deeply impressed by his linguistic skills. He would speak slowly in English but with an amazing spontaneous facility for thinking in the language he was speaking. On one occasion after a lunch he gave, in his private quarters in the Vatican to the Archbishop of Canterbury, he walked back with his Anglican guests to the main Vatican Palace. It had been a simple but good lunch. They had talked as fellow pastors of the problems facing the Christian Church. Whatever the official view of Rome about Anglican ministry, they had spoken as brother bishops. So as he bade farewell to the Archbishop he said: 'May affective collegiality', theological-speak for bishops working together, 'become effective collegiality.' From the affection and trust of pastors eating and talking together he was looking to the eventual unity of Christians for the effectiveness of the gospel.

Now that he is, we trust and pray, eating and drinking at the table of the Kingdom, Anglicans will continue to hope he prays for the affective unity of the church and the effectiveness of the mission of the gospel.

8

Learning from the Arts

David Brown and Ann Loades

1. Hope in pain

Although we have worked together on jointly editing some volumes on sacramental theology, this essay is our first fully collaborative independent exercise. It has been a valuable and mutually enriching exercise in which often aspects that might otherwise have been neglected have been included in our overall perspective. Indeed, our experience provides a more general parable for what we are attempting here: the suggestion that the role of religion in the arts should not be narrowly conceived. Quite commonly among Christians their role, however valuable, is narrowly circumscribed to that of illustration or confirmation of faith. To us, however, it seems that there is much more on offer: an inherent spirituality that can draw from us all a deeper understanding of the nature of our faith, and not only through contemplation of the work of specifically Christian artists. The activity of the Holy Spirit is by no means that narrowly confined. So the process of enrichment works both ways, not only from the Bible and Church to the arts but also from the arts to the Church.

In this essay we will explore two elements in the Christian faith, first the crucifixion and then the resurrection. In the latter case we want to suggest that, despite some indications to the contrary, art can help not only to retain an appropriate sense of mystery in which not all is known but also to ensure that it is a doctrine of continuing relevance to us in the present. With the crucifixion the focus will be somewhat different. While earlier generations of Christians often usurped the Cross in a spirit of triumphalism, nowadays sometimes the pain and vulnerability is so stressed to the exclusion of all else that gloom rather than hope seems almost to be the message. In our opinion neither view gets it quite right, and so we need to explore how best to express both aspects of what the Cross meant, and so offer hope in pain.

In that exploration non-belief can also make a contribution. Weekly attendance at church in England stands at roughly only 7 per cent of the population. By contrast, according to the 2001 Census, 72 per cent of the population declared allegiance of some kind to the Christian faith and 76 per cent to some kind of religion. So there is this mismatch between people who go to church and the great majority of the population, who are still interested but who have not been brought inside the church's doors (or only rarely so). It is so very easy to think that there is a hostile world out there when in fact very often God is speaking outside the Church as well as within it. God does not always speak through those of explicit faith. The message comes sometimes through those of implicit faith or perhaps of none and we need to hear them. As will become obvious, in developing our case, insights do not always come from the conspicuously devout.

To indicate that potential breadth, we want to begin with pop music. It is so easy to assume this is a totally alien territory but that is very far from being so. Suppose we go back to the 1960s, and recall those Beatles hits that so dominated the period. Not all of them by any means were simply about puppy love. Two, in particular, had a religious dimension. In 'Let it Be', Paul McCartney's tribute to his dead mother Mary, gospel rhythms were used to sing of his filial debt.[1] If in 'Eleanor Rigby' at first all one notes is the way in which Father McKenzie, the priest conducting Eleanor Rigby's funeral, is portrayed as a rather sad, pathetic figure, more sustained listening suggests more complex attitudes.[2] What the Beatles seem to be suggesting is not hostility to religion as such but something worthwhile lost, marvellously evoked by the string quintet behind the singing that speaks of a longing for the Church to be as it should be – communicating.

In that same period the other great group were the Rolling Stones, and 'Sympathy for the Devil' was of course one of their best-known songs. As a result readers are likely to conclude that they could not possibly have anything positive to do with religion, but time marches on and in the latest solo album to come from Mick Jagger, the lead singer, or as he now is Sir Mick Jagger, there are no less than three songs about religion. Here are some words from one of them, the track 'Joy' from *Goddess in the Doorway*:

Oh joy love you bring
Oh joy make my heart sing

And I drove across the desert
I was in my four wheel drive
I was looking for the Buddha
And I saw Jesus Christ

He smiled and shrugged his shoulders
And lit a cigarette
Said jump for joy
Make some noise
Remember what I said

My soul is a like a ruby
And I threw it in the earth
But now my hands are bleeding
From scrabbling in the dirt
And I look up to the heavens
And a light is on my face
I never never never
Thought I'd find a state of grace[3]

So there you have someone who seemed in earlier life to have no sympathy for Christianity whatsoever, though he did begin life as a choirboy. This does not mean Jagger has now become a Christian but it does mean that he is willing to show some sympathy to Christianity, that there might be something there after all and so we can have a dialogue. Sadly, in the contemporary Church, so far from engaging in such dialogue, we often run scared and so retreat. One worry the two of us have about the current popularity of icons in the Western Church is that, while they have important and positive things to say, they can sometimes suggest just such a Church – one turned away from the world rather than engaged with it. Certainly, we do not want to launch here a purely negative attack on another branch of the Christian Church. So what we shall do instead is examine a selection of paintings in the Western tradition and related music that raise the same sort of question, 'What is missing?' Although we have tried to produce sufficiently detailed descriptions for the essay to be read on its own, a number of possible ways of accessing the pictures are provided in the references at the end of this chapter.

First reflect on how the crucifixion has been depicted over the course of the Christian centuries. A typical example of the approach within the first millennium might be to take the Christ from the seventh-century Durham Gospels, a book still in the cathedral's possession.[4] It offers a very majestic Christ on the Cross, surrounded by angels and peering out at us interrogatively, as if to say, 'Why have you put me here?' Despite his body only being supported by the nails, there is no hint of pressure on the body whatsoever. Christ's arms are perfectly horizontal, and he even wears what is called a *colobium*, a full robe, to protect his modesty.

A similar pattern emerges in the Lindau Gospels from the ninth century.[5] Here again we discover tremendous emphasis on the transcendence of Christ. He has won a great victory over sin and death, and so the Cross is expressed in supremely confident terms, again without any obvious sense of pressure or weight on the arms. The angels weep, but not Christ himself.

That kind of theme is sometimes continued into modern art, though it is very much a minority tradition. An unusual example comes from the Jewish artist Marc Chagall, a Russian who lived most of his life in France. Throughout most of his life Chagall had a positive evaluation of Christianity. His most famous crucifixion is the 1938 *White Crucifixion*, in which he uses Christ to represent hope for his fellow Jews, even in the face of the Holocaust.[6] In 1950, however, he went even further, in *Christ*.[7] In this case one is presented with an almost smiling Christ set against a bright, starry sky. Although the people beneath weep, he does not.

A contemporary painter who reflects a similar perspective is Craigie Aitchison, born in Edinburgh, but now living in London. Although not a churchgoer, he nonetheless frequently paints crucifixions, quite often with his favourite breed of dog present, a Bedlington hound. Commonly a very positive emphasis is given to the crucifixion, with great rays of light coming from heaven down upon the Cross, with the dove of the Spirit also present,[8] and Christ, as it were, off the Cross, indicated somewhat para-doxically by Christ being deprived of his arms. He can walk free as it were, since his arms are not constrained.

All such paintings speak of hope, but the question remains: do they tell the whole story or is there something important missing, particularly in relation to contemporary society? Most contemporary art takes the view that there is.

The devout Georges Rouault is an obvious case in point. There is a much more obvious emphasis on the identification of Christ with humanity in all its suffering. Rouault, arguably the greatest religious painter of the twentieth century, was a deeply compassionate man. Many of his paintings are of people on the margins of society – clowns, prostitutes, and so on. If Christ is often bathed in a beautiful light that speaks of his divinity, there is enough of the tragedy of life portrayed to make clear his total identification with such people.[9]

Meanwhile in Germany, the Cross was being used even more forcefully by Otto Dix. Dix wrestled with his country's experience of the First World War. As the Nazis advocated a renewed militarism, Dix reflected on the suffering of men on the battlefields, where they died so fast in scrambles for another yard of mud that their bodies could not even be removed before the next wave came out of the trenches, and so they had to step over the bodies of their fallen comrades. The carnage was appalling. Dix is really raising two issues. One is 'Do we really want to go to war again?' The deeper issue is 'Where is Christ in all this?'

In his most challenging version on this theme, *The War*, one observes at the forefront of the painting someone who could conceivably be the centurion but here dressed in gas mask and tin helmet. Not far distant, Christ is hanging in a position you would not expect to find him. The dead Christ is lying upside down, with his face towards the bottom of the painting and his crown now adrift from his head. There is also another figure with pointing finger.[10]

That pointing finger alludes to the most influential painting of the crucifixion for the twentieth century, ironically painted though it was in the sixteenth century on the eve of the Reformation. The pointing figure is actually a quotation from the Isenheim altarpiece of Matthias Grünewald. That painting had a huge influence not just on numerous painters of the twentieth century but also on music. Paul Hindemith was not a believer but he wrote an opera called *Mathis der Maler*. 'Matthew the painter' takes up the various themes of Grünewald's painting and questions how we are to face evil and suffering. His opera was eventually put in the form of a symphony, which is the version commonly performed today.[11] Like Dix, Hindemith was banned by the Nazis.

The pointing finger that is quoted by Dix alludes to John the Baptist pointing towards Christ, a reminder of the permanent eucharistic significance of Christ as the Lamb whose blood is gathered in the chalice at the foot of the Cross in Grünewald's painting.[12] The most important difference from paintings mentioned at the beginning of this discussion, such as those from Durham and Lindau, is in the transformation in the position of the arms. Instead of the pure horizontal, there is now a V shape, emphasizing the acute suffering that Christ underwent for our sake. The rib cage is almost being torn apart. The overwhelming agony of those present is also obvious, among them the Virgin Mary, the Beloved Disciple, and Mary Magdalene here with her ointment jar. In the two side panels of the triptych there are two major saints, St Anthony on one side and St Sebastian on the other, the latter also a suffering figure, killed by arrows under the emperor Diocletian. The relevance of the former will become clear in a moment.

Inconceivable in first-millennium art, to this day this painting would still be regarded in Eastern Christendom as quite the wrong type of art, where it is often interpreted as an assault on the dignity of Christ's person. Certainly, the challenge it presents is profound: suffering at its most acute and dreadful. In its original context the painting addressed a period of history during which approximately a third of the population of Europe had died of the Black Death and experienced the acute suffering that went with it. That said, we can also see why Grünewald became so popular in the twentieth century, with its own terrible destruction of two world wars and of course the Holocaust.

But Grünewald did not simply paint with something general in mind. The altarpiece was actually painted for a hospital. In the medieval period there was a common disease known as St Anthony's fire, now called ergotism, a deficiency in bread that produces inflammation of the flesh and boils, graphically portrayed in one of the figures elsewhere in Grünewald's painting. If you came to the hospital as a patient that figure is what you would first see in the chapel just beyond the hospital ward, a sufferer like yourself. Grünewald's painting is in fact highly complex, consisting of three separate triptychs. If someone like themselves was what first confronted the patients, when the panels were opened out for the Mass what was subsequently seen was the same agony in Christ himself, God at one with them. This offered them some hope, but so too did the symbolism within the crucifixion itself. Not only was there the blood flowing into the chalice already mentioned, there was also the fact that, while the body was pulled downwards by its weight, the arms also stretched upwards and heavenwards, suggesting the possibility of a quite different resolution to the suffering – a fact that is marvellously portrayed in the third version which the triptych could take, in which Christ is portrayed rising from the dead in an evocative array of changing colours that merge him gradually into the sun itself.[13] Grünewald thus by no means ignored the need to demonstrate Christ's ultimate victory over sin and death, but so conspicuous has the suffering become that it is easy for the viewer, even while hearing the message of God's identification with humanity in that suffering, to suppose such negativity an inescapable element in the human lot. The result of such attitudes was that in the medieval period many a saint even imposed avoidable suffering on themselves that had no obvious benefit for others, simply in order to achieve closer identification with Christ.

So it is perhaps not altogether surprising that in modern times Grünewald has been imitated to suggest a purely negative message, one that offers no prospect of hope. For the contemporary Scottish artist John Bellany the Cross speaks only of pure negativity. Brought up in a strict religious home in a Scottish fishing village, he uses fishermen and fish to indicate the sheer oppression that religion can impose, with even the fish themselves becoming threatening, crucifixion-like figures.[14]

Another example is the person often regarded as the greatest English painter of the twentieth century, Francis Bacon, a committed atheist but nonetheless absolutely obsessed with the crucifixion. For him it indicates the meaninglessness of human life – 'all that suffering'. Intriguingly, in one work he painted some observers looking on indifferently at the suffering. Their position is such that they could be interpreted as drinkers at a bar watching the horrors on television, but equally they could be read as worshippers at altar rails.[15] The potential church context is hinted at to suggest that Christians can be just as indifferent to others' suffering as the rest of humanity.

In another[16] there is a great 'scream' from the figure on the Cross, a quotation from Sergei Eisenstein's film *The Battleship Potemkin*, where such a 'scream' is one of its most memorable images. There is also a reference to well-known paintings of the deposition from the Cross, where someone is at its head, ready to take Christ's body down from the Cross. In their place Bacon puts a dog-like figure, powerless to offer any aid to the screaming individual. Pedestrians and motorcars alike indifferently pass by, with not even the suggestion of the barbed wire of a modern prison enough to detain them. Nonetheless, that was not to be Bacon's last word.

Bacon had a lover, George Dyer, whom he did not always treat very well. Dyer came from a different social class and, unlike Bacon, was not at all well educated. Bacon often used to taunt him with his inadequacies, which of course inevitably further undermined Dyer's own sense of self-worth. While staying together in a Paris hotel for a forthcoming Bacon exhibition, Bacon for once seems to have gone much too far, and Dyer committed suicide. The result was the work popularly known as the Dyer Triptych,[17] in the central panel of which one observes Dyer entering the hotel room like a great, black, death-like shadow, while the two side panels portray the events that lead up to his death from a drug overdose, over the basin on the right and on the toilet seat on the left. The surprise is what is placed centrally above the brooding figure in the central panel: a naked light bulb hanging from the ceiling by V-shaped wire threads. It cannot be a literal representation of the light in their Paris hotel room, as by this time Bacon was already a wealthy man. So presumably it holds some special significance for Bacon himself. If one recalls his obsession with Grünewald, it seems not unlikely that we therefore have here a quotation of those V-shaped arms of Christ. The light bulb symbolizes the glimmer, the very possibility of hope, that out of the love these men had for one another and despite Dyer's death, there is something that will survive all the mess. Bacon's love for Dyer will survive, despite his own contribution to Dyer's tragic end.

As a final example of such possibilities consider the more recent work of the Scottish painter Peter Howson. Brought up a Baptist, he had lost his faith by the time he was appointed an official War Artist and sent to the battlegrounds of the former Yugoslavia. *Plum Grove* is illustrative of the change, of how he succeeded in recovering his faith through the horror rather than only in its absence.[18] In the painting a castrated, tortured man is strung up on a tree. For this new crucifixion, though, instead of John and the Virgin Mary as witnesses there are children, so accustomed to the horror that they think nothing of playing around this corpse. Yet at another level there is to be observed great beauty and richness of colour. Whereas Bacon just has that light bulb, Howson uses colour here to suggest that despite the apparent trivialization of the suffering as represented by the children, there is something beyond this. Negativity, though acknowledged, is not, as it were, allowed the last word.

Consonant with that theme is the composer Krysztof Penderecki's treatment of a similar issue in his *Threnody for the Victims of Hiroshima*.[19] Penderecki, like Peter Howson, is a Christian. Both are concerned that we face the issue of suffering and God's identification with us in suffering; hence the reason that Penderecki is concerned to evoke all the horrors of suffering to the maximal extent in this particular piece. He had in fact seen his neighbours die in the Holocaust. He was brought up in a Polish town where three-quarters of the population were Jewish. His family shared a house with a Jewish family and he saw them disappear on the railway track behind the house to Auschwitz.

Such suffering can of course be approached in a number of quite different ways. The question is whether in the end there is too much negativity in the examples we have hitherto discussed. So what we want now to do is examine how these two traditions can be most effectively combined – the transcendence of suffering that was emphasized in our earlier examples and the horror that seems at times to overwhelm our later illustrations. Both aspects should be there, but somehow in a way that invites the viewer beyond the complete reality of the suffering into implicit or even explicit awareness that rather more can be said on the matter.

That this is no idle possibility is well indicated by Michael Ramsey's favourite painting. He acquired a copy of the painting in question while he was still a student at Cambridge and then kept it through nineteen house-moves and always had it in his study. Although it is a Renaissance painting by Perugino, the *Galtizin Triptych*,[20] it is very much in the first-millennium tradition of the suffering of Christ minimized. So there is a rather radiant figure on the Cross: the body remains beautiful, the arms are not pulled down and there is little sense of the rib cage being torn apart. Mary's suffering is restrained, as is that of the Beloved Disciple. But in each of the two side panels there is a penitent: Mary Magdalene on one side, with her ointment jar, and St Jerome on the other, holding a stone with which to beat his breast. The whole scene is in fact carefully integrated to suggest that from penitence we can be carried through suffering into the radiant transcendence that is Perugino's final message – the victory over suffering and death that is represented in the central Christ figure. If careful attention is given to the side panels, what one observes in the one case is a path on which Jerome's lion is leading us upwards into the brilliant landscape and radiant body of Christ that is at the very centre of the triptych. Similarly, on the other there is an open gate behind the penitent Magdalene, taking us to the sky and then the radiant Christ whom the viewer is being invited to join.

That positive emphasis also comes in pop music. A track from the Irish pop group U2's album *All That You Can't Leave Behind* has a similar, radiant message to that of Perugino:

Grace, she takes the blame
She covers the shame
Removes the stain
It could be her name

Grace, it's a name for a girl
It's also a thought that changed the world
And when she walks on the street
You can hear the strings
Grace finds goodness in everything

Grace, she's got the walk
Not on a ramp or on chalk
She's got the time to talk
She travels outside of karma,
Karma, karma
She travels outside of karma
When she goes to work

You can hear the strings
Grace finds beauty in everything[21]

Three of the four members of this group are practising Christians. There is an interesting lesson to be learnt from their history. A conservative Evangelical group in Dublin (called the Shalom group), having effected their conversion, then sought to control the general direction of the singers' lives. The result was a huge dilemma for the young men as to whether they should continue singing: whether it was compatible with their newfound faith to be pop stars. Their music was very nearly lost to the wider world, and all because some of our fellow Christians could not conceive of Christian values being communicated in a quite different context, one in which integration with the wider secular culture was taken seriously.

That integration with the wider culture is seen in Stanley Spencer's art. Born into a Methodist family, he eventually became an Anglican, and there he remained despite all the traumas and difficulties of his personal relationships, particularly with his two wives. He set many of the scenes of Christ's life in his native village of Cookham in Berkshire. If you pay a visit to the village today, you can actually follow a route known as the Spencer Walk, where the guidebook indicates the various settings against which Spencer placed the incidents from Christ's life that he painted. On the whole he avoided painting the crucifixion. However, when he did, there can be some interesting results. In the best known of these[22] we view Christ from the back of the Cross. As one's eye travels up the wood, Christ's head is finally encountered, looking heavenwards. Although Christ is clearly suffering, that heavenward look ensures that the overall message is positive. Indeed, more frightening are the implicit hints to the viewers that it is ordinary men and women who put him there. Thus the agents of the crucifixion in this painting are ordinary lads from the local brewery, wearing their characteristic red working caps. More difficult to see is the woman stretched out at the foot of the Cross, obviously totally overwhelmed by Christ's pain. It is almost as though Spencer wants to suggest that ordinary humanity is all too easily pulled in one direction or the other – to such suffering or the cruelty of the brewery workers – and that the more difficult lesson to learn is to see beyond both towards the transcendent, as Christ does with his gaze.

A particularly unusual way of making the same point is offered in a fifteenth-century book illustration (from the *Rohan Book of Hours*)[23] where initially all one notes is the absolute horror of it all, with all the figures including Christ himself apparently overwhelmed. But further observation discloses a different message. The artist has literally feathered the sky, to suggest the pervasive presence of the Spirit. The feathery, star-filled sky suggests that God will win through in the end.

But how does all this relate directly to us today? A common artistic form of making the connection in the past was through the Eucharist, and that can stand us in good stead today. Grünewald's triptych, for instance, had the lamb at the foot of the Cross receiving the blood into a chalice which could then be offered in the Eucharist. The same point is made in Raphael's adaptation of the Perugino painting discussed earlier. Raphael was in fact Perugino's pupil, and in his version, now focused into a single painting[24] rather than a triptych, the similarities with the four figures that Perugino had included in his version are obvious. If anything, in this respect Raphael is less successful than his master. Where he succeeds is in suggesting the permanent significance of the event. Perugino had already hinted at this by including a figure from a different historical age – St Jerome. Raphael carries the process further. Not only do angels catch the blood spurting from Christ's wounds in eucharistic chalices, but also the presence of Sun and Moon is indicated, to underline the event's cosmic significance. Suffering and other negative experiences are denied the last word. The radiant body and landscape merge with these other symbols to suggest a profound hope for the future.

It was a theme that was taken up in the twentieth century by Salvador Dalí, as can be seen in his 1955 *The Last Supper*.[25] This painting occupies a prominent position in the National Gallery of Art in Washington, DC, in the main passageway between the two main buildings of the gallery. So it is a painting every visitor to this gallery sees. Dalí had in fact been brought up by an atheist father, and was himself an atheist in his earlier life. During this time he produced some works that can scarcely be described as anything other than blasphemous, such as his *Profanation of the Host*. But during the course of the Second World War he began to change his mind and after the war he became a practising Roman Catholic. He thought, however, that Grünewald had gone in quite the wrong direction, and indeed spoke of 'the materialistic and savagely anti-mystic Christ' of Grünewald. He explained that he wanted to try to use a quite different sort of image in order to indicate what he thought the crucifixion was really all about.

So in this particular painting he has the human Christ pointing a finger heavenwards at a larger version of his body which presides over the whole scene. Although this larger figure is clearly intended to allude to the crucified Christ, the arms are more horizontal than vertical. In other words, the suffering is not emphasized, and indeed, if anything, the hands seem to be pointing downwards by way of blessing. So the significance of the crucifixion is the blessing that it brings. Note too his way of trying to bring out the permanent significance of the crucifixion. The Last Supper has in effect been transformed into a celebration of the Mass, with the figures of the disciples made to look more like priests, wearing as they do albs and kneeling as they might before the consecrated host.

It is a related message that emerges from Britain's best-known Dalí painting, *Christ of St John of the Cross*.[26] This is in the St Mungo's Gallery of Religious Art in Glasgow. Although the crucified Christ who looks down from heaven has worn hands, it is a radiant body that is giving the world below its blessing. A contemporary relevance is achieved through the inclusion of a fishing boat that reminds us of Dalí's own native village of Port Lligat in Spain. The purchase of the painting was hugely controversial at the time because of how much Glasgow City Council had paid for it. So, when it was first put up for pubic display, people in their thousands went to see it. Their reaction surprised the art critics. Many took their hats off and stood there in total silence.

A fitting conclusion to what we have been trying to say can be provided by reference to yet another piece of music, this time by Ralph Vaughan Williams. He had an ambiguous and often problematic relationship with the institutional church but was crucial for the publication of *The English Hymnal* at the beginning of the twentieth century. He also produced some remarkably fine musical settings of great religious poetry, among them five of George Herbert's poems, gathered under the title *Five Mystical Songs*. Perhaps the most beautiful is 'Love Bade Me Welcome'.[27] Although George Herbert was in some ways a reluctant priest, believing himself emotionally and intellectually unsuited to the priesthood, there is no doubt about the depth and sincerity of his faith. If Vaughan Williams sat more uncomfortably on the edge, he does succeed marvellously in entering into the spirit of Herbert's poetry. Secular and sacred thus combine to deepen the message of Christ's cross and its permanent relevance to our lives. Vaughan Williams' matchless setting of this particular poem gives us time to take in the depth of Herbert's perception, as the singer unhesitatingly identifies the one who summons him with gentle persistence as the loving Christ. As a sinner his emotional distress at his own unkindness and marring of Love's work is expressed through changes of key and vocal crescendi. But the final transition to a burden-free acceptance of Love's invitation comes with the advent of a serene choir. As their voices fade, an instrumental ensemble is introduced to represent the courteous joy of the Eucharistic feast.

In the first part of the essay we have been concerned to emphasize the capacity of works of art, secular no less than sacred, to enrich our faith, to suggest that the wider culture, so far from being antithetical to Christianity, can in fact help us on our pilgrim way. In doing so, inevitably it has been necessary to expound meanings rather than invite exploration. But it is really the open-ended character of art that gives it its power. It is by contemplating a painting or piece of music that we discover their full potential, not by approaching them as though their role was purely illustrative, with everything really known in advance as it were. The work of artist and composer are at their best, not when they offer immediate answers, but rather when viewers and listeners are forced to think further and reflect. Drawn in initially perhaps by a powerful expression of suffering, more detailed consideration then opens up the new possibilities that Christian faith can offer. The irony is that the hesitant agnostic or even committed atheist (like Bacon) can sometimes express this better, precisely because dogma has not taken over completely from imagination and so clouded the eyes rather than opened them to a new vision.

2. Consummation in mystery

Some readers will know that John Paul II particularly admired the work of Bob Dylan. He asked that Dylan should sing at the Eucharistic Congress that took place at Bologna in 1997, where he performed three of his songs, among them 'Knockin' on Heaven's Door'. More poetic and more profound is 'Every Grain of Sand':

> In the time of my confession, in the hour of my deepest need
> When the pool of tears beneath my feet flood every newborn
> seed
>
> . . .
>
> In the fury of the moment I can see the Master's hand
> In every leaf that trembles, in every grain of sand.[28]

How best to evoke the continuing impact of the risen Christ in the lives of Christians is also an issue to which much attention has been given over the course of the history of the visual arts. To begin with there was considerable hesitation about any form of direct representation of Christ's life in art. The last area to be yielded, as it were, was in fact the resurrection; so of all the main elements in the story of Christ, direct representations of the resurrection are the latest. The earliest forms are consistently allusive. An obvious example is the so-called *Two Testaments Sarcophagus*, in which Daniel in the lion's den is substituted for any more explicit way of identifying Christ's res-urrection.[29] But by the later Middle Ages literalism had com-pletely superseded that earlier hesitancy, and so, intriguingly, the same museum that now houses Grünewald's crucifixion triptych also contains a representation of the resurrection by Martin Schongauer that could scarcely be more prosaic. Christ literally steps out of the tomb.[30]

The question that needs to be addressed is whether such a direct approach is not in the end counterproductive. Literalism, so far from overawing us, actually increases our doubts. Such por-trayals make the resurrection look all too pedestrian, too pedan-tic, as Christ steps nonchantly beyond death, raising his fingers to bless, and even carrying his own battle standard.

In the estimation of modern art historians Schongauer will always remain a minor figure. So perhaps a better indication of how deep the problem runs would be to take someone well represented in the National Gallery in London, Piero della Francesca. His por-trayal of the resurrection, though elsewhere, is justly famous.[31] Christ is made to emerge in much the same way as Schongauer's Christ, but there the difference ends. Piero offers us an extraordi-narily powerful face and body that seems effortlessly to dominate the sleeping soldiers beneath. Yet even so the same question arises, whether the artist has truly captured what is significant about the resurrection. Is there not something vital missing, something more than the mere return of Christ from the dead?

That more, we suggest, is to be found in a drawing from Windsor Castle by Michelangelo, 'The Risen Christ'.[32] It was included by the Queen in the millennium celebration tour of paintings and drawings owned by the monarch. Here any attempt at literal representation is deliberately abandoned as the price that has to be paid if the deeper realities behind what is taking place are to be brought out. So, significantly, rather than stepping out of the tomb Michelangelo's Christ actually pushes heaven-ward more in the manner of an ascension than a resurrection. The body is also deliberately made as beautiful as possible, pre-sumably to symbolize the transcending of death. What we are being invited to consider is the possibility that a transformed soul can lead to a transformed body, one that (metaphorically) is able to soar heavenwards and so enter, under God's grace, new dimensions that transcend any purely material restraints.

The irony is that such wider possibilities are sometimes better identified by those outside the faith. Like Dylan, Jacob Epstein was an American Jew. Unlike Dylan, however, he never converted to Christianity. Instead, although he became a naturalized Englishman, he continued loyal to his Jewish roots. His 1919 sculpture *Risen Christ* is a triumph of the kind of perceptivity we have in mind.[33] Initially the sculpture may suggest purely conventional elements. For instance, with one hand Christ points to his other hand, indicating the terrible cost of what he endured (in Epstein's case broadened to include all those who had suffered as a result of the First World War). Symbolically, however, he is attempting something rather more, to indicate that the sufferings are those of someone who is more than merely human, that divinity itself is present here as the two realities of heaven and earth become inextricably linked. The connection is made partly by one hand pointing heavenwards, but more importantly through the artificial lengthening of Christ's body. Careful scrutiny of its dimensions forces the admission that this is an impossibly long human body, with any normal legs required to stop far short of where they actually do. Its very length suggests a body thrusting heavenwards, while the pointing finger seems to invite us to join in that same movement.

That a symbolic approach from a Jewish artist should be more effective at conveying the realities of the Christian faith than more literal treatments by Christians reminds us that divine grace does not always act in expected ways. Ironically, precisely because non-believers are more likely to maintain the element of mystery (they are not quite sure what happened), their efforts meet with more success. It is particularly sad, therefore, to recall how much anti-Semitism was involved at times in the reception of Epstein's work. Father Bernard Vaughan, a Roman Catholic priest, led a major campaign against him ever being allowed to do representations of Christ. He was fiercely supported by some newspapers, but fortunately some Christians ranged themselves on the other side, among them the future Archbishop of Canterbury, Cosmo Gordon Lang.

When we described the Grünewald triptych, readers will recall that we talked about the way in which, as the patients were being brought into the hospital, they would see one image and then the panels could be opened up for them to see a quite different but related image. In that context our stress was rightly on the image first of their own suffering and then that of Christ sharing that suffering with them. But there was a third image available that was no less important. Since, despite the care they were offered in their suffering, many of them would die in any case, it was important that they should see the possibility of the complete transcendence of death, the complete transcendence of pain. This Grünewald offered in his image of the resurrection. Here too there is no surrender to literalism. Gradual emergence from the tomb or overawed soldiers play no role. Instead, as in Michelangelo's drawing the image is one of heavenly flight with the colours that surround him merging into those of the Sun. Christ becomes as it were the glory and radiance of the Sun, surely an altogether more successful way of conveying to the tormented hospital patients the restoration that might be theirs in another life than either Schongauer or Piero della Francesca could achieve by their approach. They after all still left it uncertain what relevance the event had for the observer, whereas by using the image of the Sun Grünewald leaves us in no doubt. Just as its rays brighten and warm our lives, so too can Christ's resurrection.

For a quite different contemporary example, consider a sculpture from twentieth-century North America, *Resurrection II* by Paul Granlund in the Episcopal Cathedral in Minneapolis.[34] Another image of taking flight, this time it is as though Christ is himself treated as a bird, already bursting out of the box that contains him in order to spread his wings and so take flight. Not of course that art need be painting or sculpture to make the point. Anyone who watches ballet or has studied pictures of dancers will be aware of how often jumps in the air function as metaphors for transcendence. Of course no more may be expressed by this than feelings of exhilaration, the kind of 'high' or joy one might get in gymnastics through being airborne. But at other times ballet choreographers clearly intend something more, not necessarily religious but at the very least on the verge of such ideas, of moving to a new sphere or new level of existence. Photographers can catch dancers in mid-flight, and so in some ways make the point even more effectively. So one way of engaging our imaginations on the theme of the resurrection might be to browse a book of such images while listening to a related piece of music such as the dance chorale the contemporary Scottish composer James MacMillan wrote on the Easter theme for his piece *Veni, Veni Emmanuel.* As it is an instrumental piece, neither it nor balletic images need necessarily evoke thoughts of Easter, but our suggestion is that they often will do so for the Christian precisely because Christ's actual resurrection is in any case beyond adequate description and so one can only begin to get there by analogy, by thinking laterally. So music or image that hints at a capacity on our part under God's grace to become otherwise than what we now are can begin the sort of reflection that may draw us towards engagement with the more radical kind of transformation that is suggested by Christ's resurrection. In MacMillan's piece the recurring drumbeat in the background emphasizes the continuing beat of Christ's heart that we are now invited to dance to.[35]

As a matter of fact none of the Evangelists describe the actual moment of resurrection. So, although numerous artists have tried to do so, it perhaps comes as no surprise that more often in the history of art it is to the resurrection encounters that artists have turned rather than to the event itself. A case in point is the Supper at Emmaus, of which Caravaggio painted two, one of which the National Gallery in London now owns.[36] It depicts the moment of discovery of the risen Christ. The shock of recognition on the faces of the two disciples on either side is quite obvious, as is the puzzled look of the innkeeper standing behind and looking down on Christ's beautiful face. But Caravaggio is determined that we should not simply interpret it as an encounter that took place two thousand years ago. To achieve some present involvement on our part as spectators, he deliberately extends the arms of one of the disciples into our space. His elbow juts out alarmingly, as though about to nudge us in the ribs, while the tablecloth seems almost to totter over the frame and pour its basket of fruit into our lap.

There is a fashion at the moment that wants to make Caravaggio into someone who is really only interested in artistic devices, who was really hopelessly promiscuous and without any religious commitment. It is a view that was popularized in Derek Jarman's 1986 film *Caravaggio* about the artist but there is actually remarkably little evidence in its support. It is certainly true that Caravaggio did kill a man (probably accidentally), and that does seem to reflect a violent life. But to deduce from such violence and visits to prostitutes that he was without a shred of Christian belief is a dangerous game. Human beings are seldom quite that simple. But even if it were proved one day that this was so, it still would not detract from our conviction that he remains a great and profoundly Christian artist. This is precisely because he is not just concerned to evoke a scene from the distant past. He knows that to speak truly of resurrection he must bring Christ into the present, and he does this not only through the devices already noted but also in numerous other symbolic references that speak of Christ's continuing presence in the Eucharist. Not only is bread present but even grapes, which would have been out of season at that time of year.

To us, however, it is his second and less familiar version of this scene that is the more profound.[37] Now in Milan, it suggests a deeper, more reflective faith, with psychological, more inward issues now to the fore. Whereas in the earlier London painting, despite the disciples' torn clothes, we were still in a relatively wealthy inn (as the quality of the tablecloth and its spread clearly indicate), now Christ sits at a very obviously poor table. He looks much more reflective, almost sad, but that is matched by the intensity of the devotion with which the disciples look at Christ. So Caravaggio is now trying to encourage our engagement through such a gaze of devoted commitment rather than, as it were, in the stage props of the earlier painting.

Caravaggio's two paintings are based on Luke, while Epstein's *Risen Christ* is derived from the incident in John 20 where Christ offers Thomas his wounded hands and side. Perhaps, however, the most painted incident also comes from John 20, Mary Magdalene's encounter with the risen Christ that includes those extraordinarily mysterious words: 'Touch me not; for I am not yet ascended' (John 20.17). Apart from her cure and the mention of her presence at the crucifixion, this is in fact the only major encounter that is given detailed treatment in a Gospel. It is not much on which to base any remarks about her. The Western Church, however, pursued a quite different course. Thanks to some confusion in the biblical narratives themselves, already by the beginning of the seventh century Pope Gregory the Great had produced a composite figure out of various women, including the sinner who washes Jesus' feet and Mary the sister of Martha and Lazarus. The result has been a continuous stream of reflections on what her story might mean for Christian discipleship, in poetry as well as paint, and more recently in novels and films produced by non-Christians as well as Christians. A pertinent, familiar recent example would be Tim Rice and Andrew Lloyd-Webber's piece about her from the latter's musical *Jesus Christ Superstar*, in the song 'I Don't Know How to Love Him':

> I don't know how to love him
> What to do, how to move him
>
> . . .
>
> Should I bring him down?
> Should I scream and shout?
> Should I speak of love, let my feelings out?
> I never thought I'd come to this – what's it all about?
>
> . . .
>
> He scares me so
> I want him so
> I love him so[38]

The result is many millions introduced to the Christian gospel but in a way that for some may seem controversial or even unwanted (because of the sexual element). Such reactions are a pity because interest and engagement with the question of Christ's potential significance is unlikely to come for all people in the same way, and indeed sometimes, as we have already noted with Epstein, it is those on the fringes who are the more perceptive in recognizing a wider range of possibilities. That is arguably the case with those lyrics of Tim Rice that have been set to Andrew Lloyd-Webber's music.

Go back almost half a millennium, and one discovers an equal concern among artists to avoid the merely descriptive. One of the finest works in London's National Gallery is Titian's *Noli Me Tangere*.[39] Painted in 1515, it tries to capture that moment when the risen Christ rebukes Mary by saying 'Don't touch me' or perhaps better, 'Don't hang on to me'. Modern radiation techniques have discovered that in its first version Titian had portrayed Christ wearing a gardener's hat, but he must have thought that too crude or literalistic, as it was certainly abandoned in due course, as was the original angle of Christ's head, which had been turned away from her. Now instead we are offered a moment of great intimacy between them. Absent too are those terrible banners of victory that could so easily suggest the endorsement of the Crusades or other wars. Now, as they look into one another's eyes, he draws back but in a way that also suggests invitation. While her hand on the ointment jar deflects one's eye to the bottom of the painting, once there it is soon drawn upwards by the angle of her body, up from the tip of her splendid robe through the interchange between them into the sky with the arching tree, allowing them both, as it were, to appear to ascend heavenwards. Intriguingly, during the Second World War, when the paintings of the National Gallery were taken away for safe storage and the public were given the opportunity for one or two to take turns on exhibition, this was among the first to be selected. Apart from the quality of the art, what seems to have attracted such a judgement was an implicit sense of the ability of the painting to speak to a condition of pain and grief and loss and suggest how contact might be retained with the people one loved, even though one might never see them again in this life.

Quite different is the manner in which Graham Sutherland chose to represent the same scene. Now best known for his work at Coventry and for his stark *Crucifixion* that stands opposite Henry Moore's *Mother and Child* in the parish church of St Matthew's, Northampton, his resurrection encounter is also a product of patronage by the same priest who had encouraged the earlier work at Northampton. Walter Hussey, now Dean of Chichester, commissioned the work, the two versions of which can still be seen at Chichester, one from Hussey's own collection given to the Pallant House Gallery[40] and the other in the cathedral itself.[41] The earlier version also once had a gardener's hat that was subsequently abandoned. This time, however, instead of the exchanged gaze and the angle of body and tree suggesting the whole movement of both Christ and Mary into a new dimension, there are more obvious props such as the ladder, with the pot plants helping to conjure up the notion of a garden. If that may seem to indicate a more pedestrian imagination, the ladder is not left to do all the work on its own. The back of Mary Magdalene's feet and the whole thrust of her body is in any case in movement upwards. Also, putting Mary in contemporary dress (possibly that of a contemporary London streetwalker) stresses the relevance of what is happening not just for Mary but also for ourselves.

For that last point, one might compare the sculpture of contemporary artist David Wynne for Ely Cathedral where Mary Magdalene is to be found in a sort of skinny, modern dress.[42] Again, initially the notion of ascent may be thought to lie simply in the direction of Christ's hand, but closer examination reveals the employment of strategies similar to those we noticed earlier with Epstein. There is the same elongation of Christ's limbs in which Mary seems to be participating.

Although all our most recent examples have been personal encounters, traditionally Christian doctrine has insisted that this is only one element in the resurrection. Equally important is its corporate dimension, the fact that it involves us all. Artists focusing on personal encounter have sought to include that other dimension by encouraging our gaze heavenwards: we too are invited to move in a similar direction. But more explicit appeals are of course possible. An example from contemporary pop music is to be found in some of the lyrics of Bruce Springsteen, the rise in whose popularity intriguingly coincided with a corresponding decline in that for Bob Dylan. Like Dylan he is an American but from a quite different family background. He had been brought up a Roman Catholic, and quite literally had hated it. One of the nuns who had taught him as a child even put him in a dustbin under the desk, with the remark that that is all he would ever be, worthless. So not surprisingly he ended up thoroughly anti-Catholic. But, as he himself records, he still continued to wrestle with aspects of the Church's teaching, and in retrospect his albums can in fact be interpreted as a progressive exploration of the theme of redemption. He finds the presence of Christ particularly in those who take risks in loving others. So, for example, in a piece called 'Ties That Bind' he sings:

> You're so afraid of being somebody's fool
> Not walkin' tough, baby not walkin' cool
> You walk cool, but darlin', can you walk the line
> And face the ties that bind
> The ties that bind
> Now you can't break the ties that bind[43]

Or in 'Human Touch', he observes:

> You can't shut off the risk and the pain
> Without losin' the love that remains
> We're all riders on this train[44]

And so it is through the risk of loving that he has returned once more to the Christian faith. Such themes are particularly explicit in his most recent album, which is called *The Rising*. The album includes a tribute to the firemen of 11 September, in a song called 'Into the Fire':

> May your faith give us faith
> May your hope give us hope
> May your love give us love[45]

91

For him that example is significant because it is pre-eminently through others that we come to faith.

Towards the end of the album we find the theme song for the album, itself also entitled 'The Rising'. He takes us through what he calls 'stations of the cross,' ordinary human experiences of love and its trials and tribulations, towards an opening sky. Beginning with the singer's own voice this gradually gives place to the voice of Christ in what is a very interesting interchange:

> Can't see nothin' in front of me
> Can't see nothin' coming up behind
> I make my way through this darkness
> I can't feel nothing but this chain that binds me
> Lost track of how far I've gone
> How far I've gone, how high I've climbed
> On my back's a sixty pound stone
> On my shoulder a half mile line
>
> Come on up for the rising
> Come on up, lay your hands in mine
> Come on up for the rising
> Come on up for the rising tonight
>
> Left the house this morning
> Bells ringing filled the air
> Wearin' the Cross of my calling
> On wheels of fire I come rollin' down here
>
> Come on up for the rising
> Come on up, lay your hands in mine
> Come on up for the rising
> Come on up for the rising tonight[46]

This may seem a somewhat allusive way of referring to the resurrection but it does represent the work of someone who in the process of such writing has returned to the Christian faith. The influential US sociologist Andrew Greeley has in fact described Springsteen as 'the great Catholic liturgist of our time'.[47]

In our first piece we passed some critical remark on Orthodox icons. So it is appropriate to add something positive here. For if, in our view, Orthodoxy shows altogether too much reticence in portraying the agonies of the crucifixion, in its treatment of the resurrection it does at least succeed in avoiding the prevailing Western preoccupation with individualism and literalism.

It does so precisely because it never went down the path of directly representing the event. So in Greek or Russian treatments of the 'resurrection', what one finds instead is what has been variously known as the descent into hell or the harrowing of hell, the liberation of souls that had been awaiting Christ's return to life. What one usually observes is Christ stretching out his hand over a broken door, drawing Adam and Eve out or else with them already either side of him, along with the two kings David and Solomon and various other Old Testament figures. The allusion is of course to Matthew's Gospel (27.51–53), with its notion of people coming out of the tombs at the point of the crucifixion. So here it is corporate experience that is very much being stressed.

Nowadays Wassily Kandinsky is known as one of the great abstract artists of the twentieth century. A Russian who emigrated to Germany, he lived most of his life there apart from at the very end, when he moved to Paris. He never lost his Orthodox faith. Although this is not the place to develop the theme, it is in fact possible to detect his abstract art developing out of Orthodox symbolism. Only one aspect need concern us here, as in some of his semi-abstract paintings for All Saints' Day.[48] They are wonderfully confident, with numerous saints to be noted, among them St George, St Mary of Egypt, St Cyril and St Methodius. In one Elijah is to be observed on his chariot rising to heaven. An oarsman attempts a similar pilgrimage, an image that was to play a central role in his first purely abstract paintings. What all these share with the earlier tradition of icons is a great stress on resurrection or new life as a corporate experience.

Such a way of viewing the world is of course by no means entirely absent from the Western tradition. If we move West gradually, a good twentieth-century example to take might be the work of the great Symbolist painter, Alphonse Mucha in St Vitus'

Cathedral in Prague. In his very fine stained glass window in the cathedral Christ presides over a great company of saints, the Virgin Mary on one side and the Magdalene on the other and beneath them all the great saints of this part of Europe.[49] The great Czech saint, 'Good King' Wenceslas, is right there in the middle, along with his mother Ludmila and incidents from the lives of various other saints of Eastern Europe all round about. The emphasis is on the Church as a whole being summoned to resurrection, of which the saints are an obvious foretaste.

But exactly the same experience could be had more locally in of all places the restaurant of the National Gallery in London. On its walls is a composition known as *Crivelli's Garden*, painted by the Portuguese artist Paula Rego, who now lives most of the year in England.[50] She has recently completed a painting of St Margaret of Scotland for Durham Cathedral. *Crivelli's Garden* also takes as its theme the life of the saints. Easy to recognize is the contrast between Mary the contemplative and Martha busy brushing the floor. Again, a rather plump Cecilia is clearly enjoying the experience of angels playing some music to her. Rego is very insistent about the need to give greater recognition to the role of women, and that is worked out here to the virtual exclusion of male saints. Although there were Roman Catholic influences on her childhood, for much of her adulthood she has been deeply hostile to Rome, perhaps seen most clearly in her series of paintings attacking the Church's prohibition on abortion. However, in more recent years she has shown greater sympathy, and may indeed even be returning to some form of belief. Certainly, this joyous evocation of saints enters fully into the spirit of their legends. One notes, for instance, St Catherine of Alexandria trampling confidently on the emperor who tried to kill her with his sword and failed, or how, just to let us know that good will triumph in the end, the devil is depicted being carried away on a leash: he is a mere toad.

Here too of course there can be the danger of too much domesticity, of our assuming an easy familiarity with the saints, and so an element of otherness, of mystery, in the resurrection is lost, the sense that this side of the grave it will always be something that eludes our complete comprehension. But even pictures of the saints do sometimes convey exactly that notion. An especially intriguing example is to be found in the work of the French illustrator Gustave Doré, who goes back to the passage in Matthew to which we have previously referred. He portrays the risen saints already sailing through the heavens like a somewhat sinister aircraft formation, to the complete incomprehension of onlookers below.[51]

Hitherto we have spoken of all such imagery in the context of the resurrection, without making any mention of the ascension. Yet in some ways it is the latter that is Christianity's more important doctrine, for, while the resurrection speaks of Jesus' survival of death, the ascension declares the permanent exaltation of that humanity to heaven. Yet, if anything, that doctrine has proved even more difficult to represent in the visual arts.

There must be literally thousands of stained glass representations of the ascension that now produce only a wry smile rather than any serious engagement with what is supposedly taking place. Readers will be all too familiar with the sort of thing we have in mind, and there may even be something similar in their local parish church. Christ is portrayed as already rising heavenwards with most of his body concealed in clouds. His feet, however, dangle beneath the clouds, while his disciples look on in puzzlement from below.

To be fair to that tradition, it is of course depicting rather literally Luke's own description at the beginning of Acts. However, as with the resurrection, whatever precisely happened when Christ finally took his leave, a literal representation is not necessarily the best way of conveying the significance of what occurred. So that is why we are better turning to someone like the great sixteenth-century artist Tintoretto, who tries to get beyond the literal level to say something more profound.

What he offers us are extraordinarily powerful angelic figures instead of clouds lifting Christ heavenwards. These great angels with enormous wings, however, are there not just to give greater drama to the event; they are equally there to suggest that heaven is the more real world, not our own. Indeed, this world is so ambiguously and so faintly painted that the figures in the centre observing the event look almost as though they are going to merge into the landscape. They are, as it were, the phantoms, not heaven.[52]

Often today we treat the ascension as though it were a mere appendix to the doctrine of the resurrection, whereas in the history of the Church it has quite commonly been treated, and rightly so, as, if anything, the more important of the two doctrines, given that through Christ's representative role our own humanity has been permanently exalted to heaven. There, eternally now in heaven, is the humanity of Christ and with him the great company of saints who anticipate the future destiny of the Church in general. So in the encounter with Mary Magdalene it was not just some temporary coming out of the tomb to show that he was still alive. Rather, Christ, a human being like us, is now permanently available in a new kind of way. Pre-eminently this occurs in the Eucharist, for it is assuredly the ascended Christ that we encounter in that sacrament, not some earlier stage of his earthly reality. Of course it was as crucified that he sacrificed himself for our sakes, but what he offers to us now is his total reality triumphant over sin and death.

One sometimes wonders if European art has lost its ability to convey that message. Certainly some of the most powerful imagery that expresses such a reality is in our own day derived from alternative sources. An intriguing case in point is the work of the US artist Georgia O'Keefe. Someone who lost her faith and never recovered it, she even refused Christian burial on her death. Yet she greatly admired the Indian Christians of New Mexico, so much so that she succeeded in entering into the spirituality of their beliefs and wonderfully conveys what mattered to them, if not to her. Images of crosses against the rugged landscape take up one such aspect, but so too does the Mexican symbol of the ladder that unites heaven and earth.[53] Why this particular symbol mattered to the Mexican Indians was because of course it implies not only us going up to heaven but also equally the divine coming down, the total involvement of divinity with humanity, as in the scriptural story of Jacob's ladder, with angels ascending and descending on his pillow (Gen. 28.10–17) and later through Christ himself (John 1.51).

In some ways even more intriguing is the work of the Indonesian artist Bagong Kussudiardja, who uses Asian symbolism to talk about the ascension. Christ has become a swan or bird of flight that carries us ever upwards, a messenger that unites the two worlds.[54] Since both these examples are borrowing from other cultures, it would seem appropriate to end by mentioning an illustration that comes directly from an alternative culture. In one painting from Zaïre, Christ actually dances his way to heaven but in a way that takes the rest of humanity with him.[55]

In music, however, one outstanding example of someone able to celebrate the mystery of the ascension was the greatest religious composer of the twentieth century, the Frenchman Olivier Messiaen. He saw God not just in Scripture but also equally in the natural world, particularly in the beauty of bird sound, which he marvellously evokes in numerous pieces based on that sound. He is also astonishingly successful in evoking the transcendence of mountains and the way in which they can speak to us of God. But that is not where we wish to end this reflection, but rather with his compositions on the ascension. The most famous is his *Quartet for the End of Time*, which he wrote in 1940–41 while a prisoner of war.[56] It has a gradually ascending scale that takes us heavenwards. More appropriate here, though, is another piece, *Les Corps glorieux* (Bodies in Glory), which uses the ascension to stress the mysterious, corporate character of our faith.[57] What he does is seek to evoke the joy and luminosity or brilliance of the glorious body of the ascension that belongs not just to Christ but one day to us all.

One final thought. To some our attempt to engage with contemporary culture may seem commendable but wrongly focused. While engagement with contemporary art and music has its proper place, it will be said that what our discussion ignores is where the real growth in the Church is to be found, in biblically based or fundamentalist communities in which the Word or words occupy the central place. Even if this were so, it would not be true of society at large. With such prominent roles exercised by television, advertising and the Internet, it is now a commonplace to speak of us living in a visual rather than a verbal culture. Even with pop music the words are not always significant. It is the image of the artist that matters or the particular beat of the music. That is one reason why such claims about growing churches need to be treated with some caution. To attract converts they too in turn must appeal to the culture at large, and this is in fact reflected in the form that their services now commonly take. So in US churches such as Willow Creek Community Church, where attendance is in the thousands, the use of screens, strobe lighting and so forth is by no means uncommon, and that has had its impact also on evangelism in Britain. Much the same could be said for Africa. While the financial wherewithal to call upon such technological resources is not there, visual spectacle can nonetheless be seen to be central, in gesture, movement and dance. So there is certainly a need to engage with our visual culture, and learn from it as well as contribute to it.

Notes

1 The Beatles, 'Let it Be', *Let it Be* (Apple, 1970), track 6.

2 The Beatles, 'Eleanor Rigby', *Revolver* (Parlophone, 1966), track 2.

3 Mick Jagger, 'Joy', *Goddess in the Doorway* (Virgin Records America, 2001), track 2.

4 Durham Gospels, in Durham Cathedral Library, and in Michelle P. Brown, *The Lindisfarne Gospels* (London, 2003), plate 26.

In all subsequent references where a location is not specified we believe the item still to lie in private hands. Where a cathedral location is indicated in the text, and no further details are given, a visit to that cathedral is required to view the artwork in question.

In addition, please note that many galleries now have their images on the Internet, which is a helpful alternative to looking them up in books.

5 *Crucifixion*, front cover of the Lindau Gospels (*c.* 879), in Peter Lasko, *Ars Sacra 800–1200* (New Haven: 1994), p. 58.

6 Marc Chagall, *White Crucifixion* (1938), Art Institute of Chicago, in Werner Haftmann, *Marc Chagall* (New York, 1998), p. 188.

7 Marc Chagall, *Christ* (1950), in Raymond Cooniat, *Chagall* (Naefels, 1998), p. 61.

8 See Craigie Aitchison, *Crucifixion* (1988–89), Glasgow Museums and Art Galleries, in Andrew Gibbon Williams, *Craigie: The Art of Craigie Aitchison* (Edinburgh, 1996), p. 117.

9 Compare Georges Rouault, *Prostitutes* (1909), with his *Christ Mocked by Soldiers* (1932), in Jose Maria Faerna, *Rouault* (New York, 1997), pp. 16, 56.

10 Otto Dix, *The War* (1929–32), Gemaldegalerie Neue Meister, Dresden, in Eva Karcher, *Otto Dix* (Cologne, 1992), pp. 172–73.

11 Paul Hindemith, *Symphony 'Mathis der Maler'* (1934) (Decca Recording, 1992).

12 Matthias Grünewald, *The Crucifixion* (1510–16), Musée d'Unterlinden, Colmar, in Neil MacGregor with Erika Langmuir, *Seeing Salvation* (London, 2000), p. 135.

13 Ibid., p. 187. The triptych has a multiple number of paintings both on the front and the back of the wood, which means that different patterns of three paintings are possible at any time, depending on how the panels are turned on their hinges.

14 See John Bellany, *Scottish Family* (1968), in John McEwan, *John Bellany* (Edinburgh, 1994), p. 67.

15 Francis Bacon, *Crucifixion* (1965), in Andrew Sinclair, *Francis Bacon: His Life and Violent Times* (London, 1993), plate 30.

16 Francis Bacon, *Fragment of a Crucifixion* (1950), Stedelijk Abbemuseum, Eindhoven, in Luigi Ficacci, *Francis Bacon 1909–1992* (Cologne, 2003), p. 68.

17 Francis Bacon, *Triptych* (1973), in Michel Leiris, *Bacon* (Barcelona, 1987), no. 84.

18 Peter Howson, *Plum Grove* (1994), Tate Gallery, London, in Alan Jackson, *A Different Man: Peter Howson's Art, from Bosnia and Beyond* (Edinburgh, 1997), p. 78.

19 Kryzsztof Penderecki, *Threnody for the Victims of Hiroshima* (1958–61) (EMI Records, 1994).

20 Perugino, *The Galtizin Triptych: Crucifixion with the Virgin, St John and St Mary Magdalene* (1490), National Gallery of Art, Washington, DC, in André Chastel, *Art of the Italian Renaissance* (London, 1988), p. 121.

21 U2, 'Grace', *All That You Can't Leave Behind* (Universal International Music, 2000), track 11.

22 Stanley Spencer, *The Crucifixion* (1958), in Fiona MacCarthy, *Stanley Spencer: An English Vision* (New Haven, 1997), no. 62.

23 The Rohan Master, 'Hours of the Cross' (15th c.), *The Book of Hours*, introd. by Millard Meiss and Marcel Thomas (Paris and New York, 1972), plate 57.

24 Raphael, *The Crucifixion* (1502–03), Pinacotea, Vatican, in James H. Beck, *Raphael* (New York, 1976), p. 83.

25 Salvador Dalí, *The Last Supper* (1955), National Gallery of Art, Washington, DC, in Robert Descharnes and Gilles Neret, *Salvador Dali: The Paintings 1904–1946* (Cologne, 1993), pp. 488–89.

26 Salvador Dalí, *Christ of St John of the Cross* (1951), St Mungo's Gallery, Glasgow, ibid., p. 451, and in Evelyn Silber *et al.*, *The Image of Christ* (London, 2000), p. 199.

27 Ralph Vaughan Williams, 'Love Bade Me Welcome', from *Five Mystical Songs* (1911), *Five Tudor Portraits / Five Mystical Songs* (Hyperion Records, 1999), track 3.

28 Bob Dylan, 'Every Grain of Sand', *Shot of Love* (Columbia, 1981), track 10.

29 *Two Testaments Sarcophagus* (4th c.), Lateran Museum, Rome, in Andre Grabar, *Christian Iconography: A Study of its Origins* (Princeton, 1980), no. 268.

30 Martin Schongauer (1430–91), *Resurrection*, Musée d'Unterlinden, Colmar; no illustration available in print.

31 Piero della Francesca, *The Resurrection* (1450–63), Pinacoteca Communale, Sansepulcro, in Birgit Laskowski, *Piero della Francesca 1416/17–1492* (Cologne, 1998), p. 65.

32 Michelangelo, 'The Risen Christ' (1533), Royal Library, Windsor Castle, in George Bull, *Michelangelo: A Biography* (London, 1995), facing p. 281.

33 Jacob Epstein, *Risen Christ* (1917–19), Scottish National Gallery of Modern Art, Edinburgh, in *The Image of Christ*, p. 194.

34 Paul Granlund, *Resurrection II* (1973), St Mark's Episcopal Cathedral, Minneapolis, in Susan A. Blain (ed.), *Imaging the Word: An Arts and Lectionary Resource Book* (Cleveland, Ohio, 1994–95), vol. 1, p. 185.

35 James MacMillan, *Veni, Veni Emmanuel, The Music of James MacMillan* (Catalyst, 1993), tracks 1–8, esp. track 7.

36 Caravaggio, *Supper at Emmaus* (1600–01), National Gallery, London, in Alfred Moir, *Caravaggio* (New York, 1989), p. 83.

37 Caravaggio, *The Supper at Emmaus* (1605–06), Pinacoteca di Brera, Milan, in John Gash, *Caravaggio* (London, 1980), p. 81.

38 Tim Rice and Andrew Lloyd-Webber, 'I Don't Know How to Love Him', *Highlights from Jesus Christ Superstar* (The Really Useful Group, 1996), track 9.

39 Titian, *Noli Me Tangere* (1515), National Gallery, London, in Silber et al., *The Image of Christ*, p. 173.

40 Graham Sutherland, *Christ Appearing to Mary Magdalene (Noli Me Tangere)* (1961), Pallant House Gallery, Chichester, in Stefan van Raay, Frances Guy, Simon Martin and Andrew Churchill, *Modern British Art at Pallant House Gallery* (London, 2004), p. 82.

41 Graham Sutherland, *Noli Me Tangere*, Chichester Cathedral. The painting is located in the North Nave aisle and its location may be viewed on the Chichester Cathedral website (www.chichestercathedral.co.uk/primaryframes.html; click on 'Visiting Us') The brilliant scarlet used in the picture drawing the viewer down the aisle to the chapel, where the painting forms the altarpiece there. No illustration available in print.

42 David Wynne, *Mary Magdalene Recognizes Jesus on the Morning of his Resurrection* (1967), Ely Cathedral, in Peter Sills, *Ely Cathedral: A Short Tour* (London, 2005), illus. 13.

43 Bruce Springsteen, 'Ties That Bind', *The River* (Columbia, 1979), track 1.

44 Bruce Springsteen, 'Human Touch', *The Essential Bruce Springsteen*, disc 2 (Columbia, 2003), track 6.

45 Bruce Springsteen, 'Into the Fire', *The Rising* (Columbia, 2002), track 2.

46 Bruce Springsteen, 'The Rising', ibid., track 11.

47 Quoted in E. Alterman, *The Promise of Bruce Springsteen* (Boston, 2001), pp. 186–7.

48 Wassily Kandinsky, *All Saints Day II* (1911), and *Study for All Saints II* (1911), both in Stadtische Galerie in Lenbachhaus, Munich, in Michel Comil Lacoste, *Kandinsky* (Naefels, 1979), pp. 27, 113.

49 Alphonse Mucha, stained glass window (1931), St Vitus' Cathedral, Prague, in Sarah Mucha (ed.), *Alphonse Mucha* (Prague, 2000), p. 143.

50 Paula Rego, *Crivelli's Garden* (1990), National Gallery, London, in John McEwan, *Paula Rego* (London, 1997), pp. 248–71.

51 Gustave Doré, *The Doré Bible Illustrations* (New York, 1974), on Matt. 27.51–53. The illustrations were first published in 1866.

52 Jacopo Tintoretto, *Ascension of Christ* (1578–81), Scuola Grande di San Rocco, Venice, in Tom Nichols, *Tintoretto: Tradition and Identity* (London, 1999), p. 214.

53 See Georgia O'Keefe, *Ladder to the Moon* (1958), in Britta Benke, *Georgia O'Keefe, 1887–1986: Flowers in the Desert* (Cologne, 1995), p. 81.

54 Bagong Kussudiardja, *The Ascension*, in Blain (ed.), *Imaging the Word,* vol. 2, p. 202.

55 Andre Kamba Luesa, *Resurrection* (1992), in Ron O'Grady (ed.), *Christ for All People: Celebrating a World of Christian Art* (Geneva, 2001), p. 143.

56 Olivier Messiaen, *Quatuor pour la Fin du Camps* (EMI, 1991), track 8.

57 Olivier Messiaen, *Les Corps glorieux* (1939), esp. 'Joy and Splendour of the Bodies in Glory' (Regis, 2001), track 10.

9

'Do You Love Me?'

Philip North

We begin by hearing some words from St John's Gospel, the reading used earlier today at the funeral of Pope John Paul II:

> When they had finished breakfast, Jesus said to Simon Peter, 'Simon son of John, do you love me more than these?' He said to him, 'Yes, Lord; you know that I love you.' Jesus said to him, 'Feed my lambs.' A second time he said to him, 'Simon son of John, do you love me?' He said to him, 'Yes, Lord; you know that I love you.' Jesus said to him, 'Tend my sheep.' He said to him the third time, 'Simon son of John, do you love me?' Peter felt hurt because he said to him the third time, 'Do you love me?' And he said to him, 'Lord, you know everything; you know that I love you.' Jesus said to him, 'Feed my sheep.' (John 21.15–17)

No doubt a psychologist would have one of those vile, imagination-killing bits of jargon for that wonderful resurrection scene from St John's Gospel. They would call it closure. You can just hear it. Following the trauma of the denials, Peter and Jesus repair their relationship, so now Peter can put the whole incident behind him and move on. What nonsense! This is not about closure. This is the beginning. This is the starting point of all Christian ministry. If we followed the Jewish practice of wearing passages of scripture about our person, this story should be attached to the body of every single priest.

'Do you love me more than these?' Jesus asks. He uses the word αγαπαώ. Perhaps here 'prefer' might be a better translation. 'Do you prefer these boats, these nets, this fishing to me?' And Peter replies, φιλώ. I love *you*! I love *you* passionately. He does not offer what Jesus asks. He offers more. Jesus asks again: do you prefer me? Αγαπαω. Again Peter offers more. I love you. And then the third time, Jesus too uses the word φιλώ. 'Do you love me?' And Peter replies, yes Lord, 'you know that I love you'. And now Jesus does know. Now he knows that Peter can offer the total commitment that he asks. He is reconciled, and because he is reconciled he can go out to minister. 'Feed my sheep.' 'Tend my lambs.'

'Lord, you know I love you.' It is that passionate love and that delight in being reconciled that enables Peter to minister in the name of Christ. In that love, and only in that love, can he lead and teach and evangelize. Only in that love can he suffer; imprisoned, flailed, abused, crucified. 'Lord, you know I love you.'

And so for us. 'Feed my sheep,' Jesus says to you and to me. On our sinful, weak shoulders has been laid that awesome task of tending Christ's flock. How on earth can we possibly do it? 'Lord, you know I love you.' Only through that passionate, desperate love for Jesus can we possibly hope to minister in his name.

All too often the baptized have been let down by priests who have lost that first love. Perhaps they have come to see their vocation as a career ladder rather than as a joyful self-offering to God. Perhaps greed or selfishness or the power of materialism has clouded their sense of call. Perhaps their disillusion with the institutional church has blocked the way of love and they have allowed anger and bitterness to be their motivating factors. Perhaps faith has become for them more a matter of professional necessity than a lively friendship with the living God. Jesus says to us, as he said to Peter, 'Do you love me?' Do you love me more than all this? Do you love me more than all these temptations and problems? Because only if you do can you begin to tend the lambs.

This holy ground calls us back to that first love. Here world-weary, tired priests and people are inspired by the example of a young girl. In reckless love, in joyful obedience Mary gave her body to be God's dwelling place. Mary gave her whole life as a sacrificial offering to him. That beautiful 'yes' which seems to hang in the air in this little shrine[1] reminds us of who we are called to be. Mary's transparency as a vessel of God points us to our own vocation, for only when we love as Mary loved can we feed the flock entrusted to our care.

Now, like countless millions of pilgrims for nearly a thousand years, we go to receive the waters of the well. As we are washed in this water so we are reconciled to God and brought back to our first love.

'Do you love me?' Jesus asks as we are given a sip of water from the well to drink. For he loves us so much that he has come to make his home in us and his love wells up like a fountain within our hearts.

'Do you love me?' Jesus asks as the sign of the Cross is made with water upon our forehead. For he loves us so much that on the Cross he gave his life that we might be reconciled to him, and through the power of the Cross made available to us through baptism he has called us to be with him in love for ever.

'Do you love me?' Jesus asks as water is poured into our cupped hands and splashes onto the floor. For he loves us with an abundance and a generosity that is limitless and uncontainable.

'Do you love me more than all these?' Through this pilgrimage, may we rediscover the joy of falling in love with God, and so may each one of us be renewed in our vocation. 'Yes, Lord. You know that I love you!' 'Feed my sheep.'

Note

1 This is the Shrine of Our Lady of Walsingham, Norfolk, where the Conference Pilgrimage was held on Friday 8 April.

10

Evangelization and Mission

Paul Richardson

Father Lowder's inspiration in starting the Society of the Holy Cross was the life and work of St Vincent de Paul, the French priest who lived at the end of the sixteenth and the beginning of the seventeenth century and who was concerned both with charitable works of mercy and with preaching and evangelism. To further the first objective, St Vincent de Paul started the Sisters of Charity; to promote the second, he started a religious order for men. When Fr Lowder and five other priests founded SSC, they set the new organization three aims: to encourage a stricter rule of life among the clergy; to establish home missions among the poor; to publish literature defending Catholic faith and practice. Father Lowder's interest in mission was stimulated by a fellow curate in Somerset who went on to become Bishop of Grahamstown in South Africa and who inspired Lowder to offer his services to the great Bishop Selwyn of New Zealand. In those days it took two years for a reply to reach England from New Zealand and by then Lowder had taken up a post at the Axbridge Workhouse. His experiences there helped to confirm the opinion he had formed from his work as a curate among farm labourers in his first parish: the underclass of Victorian England was in many ways just as much in need of missionaries as the Maoris of New Zealand.

Today Fr Lowder's realization that England is a mission field is much more widely held. While a religious revival is spreading through such parts of the world as Africa, Latin America and the Pacific, the pews are emptying in Western Europe and Australasia. No longer is mission an activity directed from the North to the South or from the West to the rest; it is from everywhere to everywhere. In such a situation, where mission is a worldwide activity calling for global partnership and cooperation, a worldwide body like the SSC has certain strengths and a contribution to make even though much remains to be done to establish the Society among priests outside the West. I would like to look at the problems and possibilities in mission, to consider some of the chief obstacles and ways of overcoming them, drawing inspiration from the life of Fr Lowder. Although I shall use the word 'mission', strictly speaking I am going to be concerned about that aspect of mission which is more properly referred to as evangelization. 'Mission' is taken to refer to all the tasks God sets for the Church in the world; evangelization more narrowly refers to the proclamation of the gospel, though ultimately the two cannot be kept apart. But first we need to summarize the message. What is the gospel we are trying to preach?

Some years ago Bishop David Jenkins tried to sum it up in a single sentence: 'God is,' he proclaimed, 'God is as he is revealed in Jesus and therefore there is hope.' Yes, there is more to be said, for example, about sin, repentance, or the Church but let us stick for a moment with this simple affirmation. Do modern men and women want to hear it? Are they not desperate to preserve their autonomy and independence? Some would claim that the last thing many people want to hear about is a message of God's love and the hope this gives.

Dig a little deeper, however, and you will discover hope is a commodity that is often in short supply. In many developing countries it is hard to keep hope alive in a situation where poverty and widespread disease are combined with corruption and political incompetence. In many Western countries there is evidence that people are unwilling to watch the news because they find a catalogue of disasters about which they can do nothing just too depressing. 'I don't see the point,' a young woman who refuses to watch the TV news explains to her boyfriend, who is a reporter in Pat Barker's novel *Double Vision*. 'There's nothing I can do about it. If it's something like a famine, OK you can contribute, but with a lot of this there's nothing anybody can do except gawp and say "Ooh isn't it awful?" when really they don't give a damn.'[1]

When the tsunami struck South-east Asia at the end of last year and terrible pictures appeared on television screens, it caused a debate in the Western media about the existence of God. I heard less about this debate in South-east Asia. Many people caught up in the disaster announced it was their faith that had enabled them to keep going. About this time, the two French journalists held hostage in Iraq for four months described how they had returned to the practice of their Christian faith in captivity and drawn strength from this. It should come as no surprise that researchers at Oxford University have come up with findings suggesting that faith helps people to cope with adversity.

Faced by a terrible cholera epidemic in East London, Fr Lowder did not give up and fall into despair. His faith enabled him to continue ministering to victims, making sure that the sick went to hospital, the dead were removed and buried, and infected bed-clothes were quickly burnt.

In his own mission statement, Christ declared his calling was to proclaim good news to the poor, release to captives, sight to the blind, liberty to the oppressed (Luke 4:18). It is that mission of hope and salvation in which he seeks to enlist all his disciples. The resurrection is the promise that one day that mission will be brought to fulfilment. We walk the way of the Cross confident of the glory that lies ahead.

The gospel message is one of hope and promise even if too often it is heard as one of condemnation and judgement. But let us not delude ourselves. Even if people grasp the message there are a number of factors influencing them to reject it. Three in particular call for attention. In the first place there is the post-modern suspicion of any claims to know the truth. Religion, it is thought, deals with matters that are beyond our ability to understand. Many faiths put forward claims; how can we decide between them? Should we even try to do so when commitment

often leads to conflict and bloodshed? Monotheism, it is sometimes claimed, should come with a health warning.

In the second place, and at the opposite end of the spectrum,
are those who react against the complexities of modern life
by turning to a narrow fundamentalist creed. This is the easiest
defence against change and insecurity, a way for global citizens
who still retain their tribal souls to find a sense of identity. All
across the world today, fundamentalist creeds of one sort or
another are growing. Mainstream Christians are caught between
the proverbial rock and the hard place: on the one side an alternative spirituality that promises inner peace and release from
stress without metaphysics or dogma; on the other, growing religious bodies with very clear boundaries that know not only what
they believe but also who the enemies are and how they ought
to be dealt with.

In the third place there is simple indifference. Years ago a great
US church historian, Martin Marty, described the different results
of secularization. In continental Europe it led to a battle between
the Church and the forces of disbelief, a battle we see reflected
in the Don Camillo stories or the rejection of Rocco Buttiglione
by the European Union Parliament. In the United States there was
much less division. Rather than fight secularization, the churches
became more secular themselves and retained their members in
the process. In Britain and Australia secularization led to goodwill
and indifference: people feel no hostility to the Church; they still
want their parish churches to remain open but they see little
reason to enter them and join in worship.[2]

A retreat from commitment and a suspicion of claims to know
the truth, the advance of fundamentalism, and widespread
apathy – these are three major problems we all face. In different
parts of the world, they are likely to be present in different
degrees. All of them can be found almost everywhere; some of
them are stronger in some places than others. Finding a common
strategy for evangelization and mission to deal with all of them is
not easy but certain broad points can be made.

'To be a witness', Cardinal Suhard once remarked, 'does not
consist in engaging in propaganda or even in stirring people up

but in being a living mystery. It means to live in such a way that one's life would not make sense if God did not exist.' What Cardinal Suhard asks of us is not easy but he puts his finger on the form that mission must above all take in the modern world. It must be witness. People will be inspired not so much by words as by lives that witness to God. I am talking here both about individuals and about the witness of communities. Pope John Paul II's life had the quality of witness. He remained faithful to the gospel under both Nazi and Communist persecution; as Pope, he forgave the man who tried to kill him; in later life he bore suffering and approached death in true faith.

Sociologist Rodney Stark has argued that one of the main reasons why the early Church spread so quickly was because Christians were ready to care for the victims of plague or look after the poor.[3] As well as caring for victims of cholera, Fr Lowder organized savings banks, refuges, clothing clubs, benefit societies, and numerous agencies to counter poverty. We should not write off these activities as producing 'rice Christians'. They are signs that the Church cares for people, practical but also sacramental expressions of God's love.

In affluent Western society the nature of the witness offered by the Church will be different. As far as the West is concerned, Anglicans have to ask themselves some hard questions about the identification of their Church with a particular class, a particular ethnic background, and a particular generation. All too often the phrase 'inclusive church' is taken to mean one that includes people who hold a range of fashionable liberal opinions. It does not refer to churches that embrace a wide social, ethnic and generational mix. The book of Acts tells us that it was at Antioch that the followers of Jesus were first called 'Christians' (Acts 11.26). In Martin Hengel's opinion, this is a sign that the community was perceived as having become an 'independent organization over against the synagogue community'.[4] The reason this tremendous development took place at Antioch was because it was there that believers from a non-Jewish background were first fully incorporated into the life of the Christian community. Jürgen Moltmann has even suggested that it may have been at

Antioch that the word 'church' was first used.[5] Cornelius was a Gentile and his conversion was a landmark but it was at Antioch that a more widespread and complete breakthrough into the Gentile mission took place. As a result the Christian community became genuinely inclusive. The promise of Pentecost, when Jewish converts from different parts of the world received the Spirit, was extended.

In the United States there is evidence that conservative Christian congregations are more successful at integrating people from different classes and ethnic backgrounds than are liberal congregations. This is because they are more focused on the gospel and less likely to be turned into social clubs for the like-minded. In rejecting fundamentalism, we do not want to give the impression that we have no good news to offer, no gospel to proclaim. What is crucial is that alongside proclamation there is also dialogue; as well as preaching we must be ready to listen. Mission is always God's mission, an activity the Spirit directs but in which we are invited to share as partners. As a result, he leads us in mission into strange and surprising places. The Church grows in understanding of the gospel as a result of mission. This is what makes mission so exciting; why it is different from proselytism. There are two errors to avoid. The world looks to the Church for more than an echo of fashionable opinions but at the same time there will be little inclination to pay attention to a Church that thinks it has all the answers. All the Cross-cultural missionaries I have ever met have told me they learnt more from the people they sought to serve than they were able to teach.

This same combination of dialogue and proclamation should characterize our approach to people of other faiths. Devout Muslims and Jews will not respect us for not believing our own faith and they regard relativism as amounting to a rejection of the truth-claims of all faiths, their own included. In my approach to the followers of other faiths, I make clear my allegiance to Christ as the incarnate Son of God, as the definitive revelation of God but I also believe with the late Jacques Dupuis that we can approach other religions expecting to learn from them more of Christ.

One of the reasons Fr Lowder drew thousands of people in the East End of London into the Church was because at St George's and St Peter's he offered them the experience of worship that drew them into another world and offered a foretaste of glory. Like the emissaries of Prince Vladimir of Kiev who saw the liturgy celebrated in Constantinople and reported back that now they knew God dwells with men, people entering St Peter's would wonder whether they were on earth or in heaven. Worship must be appropriate; it must be related to the context and be accessible to the worshippers; but at the present time we are in danger of confusing worship with entertainment. The secret, as one Lutheran has put it, is to reach out without dumbing down. Worship should inspire, enchant in the sense of allowing people to enter another world or, rather, to see this world through different eyes, but it must not be self-indulgent. It should issue in service and mission. The Eucharist is both an encounter with Christ and a promise and foretaste of God's coming kingdom. In the wider, secular culture we have seen an increasing use of symbols and liturgy. In the United States it has been discussed by the historian Amanda Porterfield, who sees more than political significance in such events as the burning of draft cards or the use of blood at the Pentagon by the Berrigan brothers in protests in the 1960s. To her, they mark the end of a Protestant culture that emphasized word over sign.[6] In Britain, the widespread use of candles and other signs of grief at the death of Princess Diana were seen by some as a 're-Catholicization' of our culture. Father Lowder would be astonished to see votive candles in many English cathedrals but perhaps we have not been inventive enough in taking advantage of the modern taste for liturgy and symbol.

Witness and service, dialogue and proclamation, enrichment and enchantment through worship: these are all ways in which we can respond to the challenges facing the Church's mission. But perhaps the most important point to make, both to those who fear commitment and to those who feel the attraction of fundamentalism, is that they have both alike misunderstood the nature of faith. Both sides see it as an all-or-nothing affair, a rigid set of beliefs that must be accepted without question, a decision that once made remains the same for ever. In fact the New Testament is much more a call to enter into a relationship with God through Christ in the power of the Holy Spirit. This is why God's revelation comes to us in a person, not in a set of infallible doctrines or texts. The doctrines and the texts point us to the person, the Word made flesh. Like all relationships, our relationship with God through Christ grows and develops. We see how this happened in the New Testament in the case of two great examples of faith, Mary and Peter. Both were ready to say 'yes' to God; but neither understood at first all the implications of their commitment; faith had to develop. The Holy Spirit works to help us increase in understanding but, as his question to Peter, 'But who do you say I am?', makes clear, Christ wants our faith to expand by a process of discovery and questioning. This is one reason why inculturation is so important. For people's relationship with Christ to be meaningful, the message about him has to be accessible and proclaimed in concepts that make sense to them. At the same time, as the story of Peter on the Mount of Transfiguration reminds us, we must be wary of imposing our own agenda on God and expecting him to speak only to confirm our existing beliefs and prejudices.

Faith emerges from our response to God's offer of revelation and salvation in Jesus Christ. Our relationships change us; friends, parents, teachers, heroes, role models all have an influence on us and help to make us the kind of people we are. In the same way discipleship changes us; our relationship with Christ gives us a new sense of our unique worth and value to God and helps us to see the world in a new way through the eyes of love. Christian faith does not narrow and blinker our vision; it enlarges our horizon, extends our sympathies, and challenges our presuppositions. This is why a missionary church must be a prophetic church, helping to throw the light of faith on the world and its problems in surprising ways. To go back to a point I made earlier, it is also why a missionary church must be a listening church, because not infrequently the world paid Christ more attention on certain questions than did his own followers, and truths the

Church should have acted upon have spread beyond her ranks to bear fruit elsewhere.

'Every age that is dying', taught the philosopher Boethius, 'is a new age that is coming to birth.' The same can be said of the Church. Perhaps 'dying' is the wrong word. The Church is renewing herself in the way she always has, by seeking to engage with the challenges and possibilities offered by new worldviews and cultures. The Church is forged in mission. Mission is always God's mission but he calls upon the Church to share it. Just as the Father sent the Son into the world, so the Son pours his Spirit on the Church to empower her for proclamation and dialogue, witness and service. There are many aspects of mission to which I have not directly referred. As well as evangelization, there is also the struggle for justice, peace and the integrity of creation. In a divided world, promoting reconciliation is an increasingly important Christian calling. In the end, mission involves no more and no less than sharing in God's great work of re-creation, putting back together again a world torn apart by sin, and witnessing to God's coming kingdom. We do this as Easter people, faithful disciples who believe that in the resurrection we have a foretaste and promise of the victory that lies ahead.

Notes

1 Pat Barker, *Double Vision* (London, 2003).
2 See Martin Marty, *The Modern Schism* (London, 1969).
3 See Rodney Stark, *The Rise of Christianity* (Princeton, 1996), esp. p. 161.
4 Martin Hengel, *Acts and the History of Earliest Christianity* (Philadelphia, 1980), p. 103.
5 Quoted in Stephen B. Bevans and Roger P. Schroeder, *Constants in Mission* (Maryknoll, NY, 2004), p. 27.
6 See Amanda Porterfield, *The Transformation of American Religion* (New York, 2001), esp. ch. 2.

11

Bluh, Bluh! Hail, Rejoice!

Philip North

In the sixth month the angel Gabriel was sent by God to a town in Galilee called Nazareth, to a virgin engaged to a man whose name was Joseph, of the house of David. The virgin's name was Mary. And he came to her and said, 'Greetings, favored one! The Lord is with you.'

(Luke 1.26–28)

A group of teenagers arrived at the Shrine of Our Lady of Walsingham in Easter week complete with hooded sweatshirts, baseball caps and ghastly trainers. I am always keen to be able to feign some degree of knowledge of youth culture as we approach the Youth Pilgrimage, so I started chatting. 'Tell me some of the latest youth patois', I asked them. 'For example, how do you say hello to your friends these days?' I was a bit surprised by the answer. Apparently what you do is wave your arms around in the air and say, 'Bluh, bluh!' OK, it is stupid. But at least it is joyful. So much youth jargon is dark and depressing and slightly sinister. 'Bluh, bluh!' is at least happy.

Words of greeting are so important, and perhaps that is why at the heart of the Shrine there is a place of greeting. The centre of the Shrine is not the image of Our Lady, beautiful and precious though it is to us. The centre is the Holy House, the space where the Angel greeted Mary. The word used in that wonderful greeting was the word χάιρε. It is usually translated as 'Hail' or 'Greetings' or, more accurately, 'Rejoice', all of which are worthy but perhaps slightly cold. I wonder if in today's terms 'Bluh, bluh!' might not be a better translation, because the Angel's greeting is one that is overwhelmingly joyful. And so it should be. For God has broken into his world in a way so astonishing that passionate joy can be the only response. God has taken on the form of his creation. God has become an embryo planted in the lining of the Virgin's womb. God has become human to demonstrate his love for the human race.

No wonder the Angel's greeting calls on Mary to rejoice. She rejoices as the woman whose body is to be the dwelling place for God. She rejoices as the daughter of Zion, the representative of new Israel and the one destined to be Mother of the Church. She rejoices with the joy of heaven, for through her flesh heaven and Earth are one.

But even in this delightful scene, there is darkness, a shadow. χαίρε. That word is used twice more in the Gospels. Or rather it is abused. The Garden of Gethsemane. Judas has accepted his blood money. He storms the garden with the high priest's men and finds Jesus at prayer. He rushes up and greets him – χαίρε – and so with that word he betrays him. Hours later the dithering Pilate hands Jesus to his soldiers to be flogged. They dress him in purple, they crown him with thorns and they shout at him χαίρε – hail, King of the Jews. χαίρε. That beautiful, angelic greeting. That word from heaven itself, the word that greets the Messiah. It is mangled and twisted and used to mock and betray and destroy the Son of God. And as the word of joy is abused, so the image of God in us is abused.

It is this abuse that points us more deeply than anything else to the heart of Mary's vocation. What did the Angel want Mary to do? Her call was to prepare a body for sacrifice. Her vocation was to grief and pain and confusion. Because only through her grief and her Son's sacrifice could sinful humanity be redeemed. Through Mary's obedience we are made whole and scooped up into the life of heaven.

So Mary teaches us how to rejoice. χαίρε. Hail. Now that word of delight can be on our lips as we greet the Risen Lord.

Not for us the twisted and abused version of Judas and the crowds, but as the Angel intended it. For through Jesus' dying and rising we are lifted up to God. We are part of the community of the redeemed with Mary as our mother. Our worship is one with the worship of heaven. Our joy, the joy of the Kingdom.

In a dark and cynical world, in a broken and divided Church, may we stand up and stand out as a people defined by joy. May we delight to greet the Risen Christ in all his people, most of all in the broken and the poor and the confused. And may our rejoicing make heaven present. For then, indeed, we will be the children of Mary. χαίρε. Hail! Rejoice, favoured one! The Lord is with you. Amen.

12

Stand up for Jesus

David Houlding

He saw three men in green. It was an outrage; whatever was going on? Such preposterous activity, so extreme, nothing short of popery. But the facts had had to be verified, and so it was that, in the summer of 1866, Archibald Tait, then Bishop of London, sent the Dean of Westminster, Dr Arthur Stanley, to visit St Alban Holborn, that most notorious of high churches, so that he could find out for himself whether the rumours and the reports were true. When he returned to Fulham Palace, his Lordship asked him what he had seen. He replied, 'I saw three men in green,' but wisely added and we might say, with hindsight, somewhat prophetically, 'and you will find it hard to put them down.'

And here we all are, one hundred and fifty years later, enjoying the full privileges of the Catholic faith. We have not been put down and, what is more, brothers and sisters, we are not going to be put down. Here we are and here we will remain, taking our rightful place in our beloved Church of England. Yes, today we gather as Anglican, Catholic Christians to stand up for Jesus, affirming Catholicism in the fullest sense.

So what were they doing that was so dreadful, those three men in green? What was worth fighting for? What was the point they were making? Why did they bother to go to such extraordinary lengths and at such personal risk, even to be sent to prison?

The answer of course is very simple: they were seeking to express the Christian faith in a way which would both capture and transform the hearts and minds of those they were seeking to serve. They were trying to embody the faith in ways that would speak of the glory of God. Everything they did was for the sake of mission, to bring the good news of Jesus Christ to the communities in which they ministered. The icon of our Society remains to this day that of Fr Charles Lowder. When all other professional people had fled from the area around London Docks he carried that sick child in his arms to the London Hospital.

These men ministered in some of the poorest areas of our land. They believed that Christ was to be found in the fragile brokenness of human lives, that he was there in the mess as well as in the Mass. The Mass was that point of meeting where everything was transformed and the vision of glory was realized, and still today it is true. All of us who dare to call ourselves Anglo-Catholics in the Church of England continue this incarnational ministry, recognizing the presence of Christ in each other as well as in the awesome mystery of the Mass.

We meet today at a very special moment in the Church's history as one of the greatest pontificates has just come to an end and we take our leave of one who has embodied the life of the Church on Earth in his dynamic person: Pope John Paul II.

Do you remember that great day, during his visit to these islands, when he went to Canterbury? I watched it on television. The Bishop of London, Richard Chartres, was there carrying the Cross of Canterbury in front of Archbishop Runcie. Those incredible scenes when the Pope entered the cathedral with the huge burst of applause that greeted him will always live in our memories. The challenge he presented to us was Christ's own challenge: that the Church might be one, even as the Son and the Father are one. But what has happened to that vision for unity? Can you imagine that scene happening again?

It must be our vocation as Anglican, Catholic Christians to rekindle that vision for unity that the late Pope bequeathed to us and recall the Church to the Rock from which she was hewn, that in the twenty-first century there will indeed come about that unity of all Christian people which today seems such a distant dream. To resist anything and everything that would stifle that dream or destroy that task, this is our calling. To remind the Church that her vocation to be one is her first credal hallmark. The Church's unity gives her identity and fosters her credibility in a broken and divided world. Ours is the job to make that dream come true. It is indeed a mighty task.

So how do we do it? We do it by saying what those three men in green were saying. It is not just the people at 'Stand up for Jesus' who are Catholics. It is the clergy in grey suits from that large charismatic Evangelical parish who are Catholic priests, if they did but know it. It is the low church village parson at matins in his scarf and hood who is a Catholic priest, if he did but know it. It is every single Anglican man, woman and child who are Catholic Christians, if they did but know it.

I am dissatisfied that we who know we are Catholics are content to settle with being merely a party within the Church of England. This is a shabby second-best. The claim of the Oxford Movement was that the whole Church of England is Catholic by her very nature and they started to behave like it.

We are not a national Protestant church. The Church of England, the Anglican Communion throughout the world, is part of the one holy, Catholic and apostolic Church. That is what we stand for: the Church of Jesus Christ, the Universal Church that he has called us to serve for the sake of his kingdom, so that his will may be done on Earth, as in heaven.

Our task as brethren of the Society of the Holy Cross, as Anglo-Catholics, is to stop being a party in the Church of England and to proclaim in love to each and every brother and sister Anglican that they are brother and sister Catholics too. And our task is to proclaim to the Church of England and to the Anglican Communion the truth, that she is but a part of the one, holy, Catholic and apostolic Church and that we must live, and so order our lives, in ways that are true to who we are. When the Anglican Communion opts to behave in any way that is contrary to its Catholic identity, it is being untrue to its very self.

But our identity as the Church, our selfhood, is Christ's selfhood. We are the Body of Christ. And, of course, we most fully become Christ's Body when we receive Christ's Body. And this draws our attention not inwards, but out to the world in which we live. Because, whatever else the New Testament might teach us about the Eucharist, it is clear that it is an act of gospel proclamation: we proclaim the Lord's death until he comes. This is not an activity for a chosen few, a holy huddle. As our Archbishop reminded us when he spoke to the clergy immediately before flying to Rome: 'Worship and mission are the two motors of the Church.' The bread which we break and which is the very presence of Christ has come down from heaven, to give life to the world, not just to the Church. And it is for the world that we are called to break bread, not just for ourselves. We fail in this vocation if all we do is to talk amongst ourselves. We can be good at putting up barriers and defining the boundaries, trying to create a safe space for ourselves and our like. Christ did not die to save the Church. No. He died to save the world. It is the Eucharist which makes the Church, for everyone to be saved through him for ever.

In that wonderful Gospel story of the Supper at Emmaus that we have heard,[1] the world and the Eucharist are inextricably intertwined. The Risen Christ is only recognized after the disciples have found space in their minds and in their homes for a supposed stranger. This hospitality to people who are unfamiliar or strange to us will need to be part of our Catholic, Eucharistic life too. Not for nothing did St Benedict instruct his monks to receive every guest, every stranger, as if it were Christ himself. No. We must not be clubby and introspective. My prayer for you today is that your parishes and chaplaincies will be Eucharistic communities where strangers are welcome and in them Christ will be recognized. Those strangers might be people from different parts of the world; they might be asylum seekers; they might be people who are much richer or much poorer, much cleverer or much less intelligent than you are; those strangers might be people who live a different lifestyle from yours. The Emmaus story is one of our most treasured portrayals of the Eucharistic life. It is only when the bread is broken with the stranger that Christ is recognized. Let it be our Catholic care to recognize Christ in the stranger as readily and joyfully as we recognize him in the Blessed Sacrament.

When that bread is broken at Emmaus, Christ is recognized and strangers become friends. You may know that great painting by Caravaggio called *The Supper at Emmaus*; indeed you may have seen it recently in the National Gallery.[2] It captures perfectly the scene at the supper table: the light floods down onto the table and reflects the youthful face of the Risen Christ now transformed. The two disciples are totally awestruck; their gestures are not ones which would suggest they are recoiling from the presence of the stranger in their midst. Rather they know who it is and they embrace his presence before them. The innkeeper looks on, quite clearly out of it and not understanding the significance of what is happening. The way the table is set draws us in as if we were supposed to be taking that spare place. The good food is almost falling into our laps. Jesus Christ, that stranger, is our Great High Priest and he invites us to his supper table. He is our Host and the place is set for us, it is where we belong.

Having good food on the table is, of course, quite a current theme. Was it not shocking to hear from Jamie Oliver recently that the Government spends on average the grand sum of 37p per pupil on school dinners? I spend a bit more than that on my dinner, as you might imagine. And the schoolchildren were shocked to learn from Jamie Oliver just what junk went into their favourite fast food and just how unnutritious it was.

In the Caravaggio picture, the man on the right is wearing the badge of a pilgrim. Like us, he is on the road, making his way through life. He and we need good food to sustain us on that pilgrimage of life. Christ gives us that food. It costs more than 37p. It costs no less than the life of the one who gives it. The food that Christ gives is no junk food. It is treasure, which makes friends out of strangers by drawing each to Jesus. It is Christ's very self and in it he gives us his strength and his grace to journey through life. And more than that: he feeds us with his Body so that we may become his Body, so that his work of reconciling the whole world to the Father might continue even in us, his Church, so our hearts, too, must burn within us.

Today we look back with gratitude and with some pride at the life and witness of our Catholic forebears in the Society of the Holy Cross, who knew that the Church becomes the Body of Christ when it receives the Body of Christ. Those Fathers knew too that it was in the stranger that they would meet Jesus, and their sacrificial ministry in tough parishes made the strangers to whom they ministered into friends in whom they met the Lord. Those Fathers knew that the Body of Christ was called to be one unity, not a fractured multiplicity. 'And did those feet in ancient time walk upon England's mountains green?'[3] No, they did not. But how lovely on the mountains are the feet of him who brings good news. The good news of Jesus Christ was brought to us on England's mountains green by others and it was brought to us from Rome, from Augustine, from Gregory, from Peter. Those early Fathers in the Society knew that and we know it too. We continue in the steps they trod.

Today we bear witness to all that we have received in the heritage of our Catholic movement in the Church of England. Today we restate our determination to remain true to the ideals that have formed us. How often do we fail to stand up for Jesus? The light of faith can be all too easily extinguished, and our hearts cease to burn within us. Today we commit ourselves to embrace the future with courage and determination. Whatever the future may hold, Christ is our Future. May we recognize him in the good food he gives us, in the breaking of bread. May we recognize him in the hospitality we show to one another and in our engagement with the stranger. May we hasten the day when we, as the Body of Christ, reflect his glorious Body better, when we stop turning away from our fellow Catholic Christians but come to full communion with them.

And we are called above all to love the Church and to love her Lord, the eternal high priest, who lives and reigns at the Father's right hand. He asks us to be faithful to the vision he has given us. Keeping our eyes fixed on the Rock from which we are hewn, we look once again for a new dawn for our Catholic movement.

A new universal primacy is about to begin. We live at a seminal moment. This is a crucial time for invigorating our Catholic future. With the Cross of Jesus going before us, and with him at our side, we go forward in faith, in hope and in love. Our hearts are on fire: yes, they do burn within us. We will continue to dig that pit for the Cross, to stand firm and prepare to stand out. Under God, in the power of the Cross all things are possible. In this sign we will conquer, and together we will stand up for Jesus.

Notes

1 The Gospel at Mass was Luke 24:13–35.
2 There was an exhibition of paintings by Caravaggio, including *The Supper at Emmaus*, at the National Gallery during the week of the Society's celebrations. A picture of the painting was projected on a screen during the sermon.
3 William Blake, preface to *Milton: A Poem* (1804–10).

13

Be Still and Know That I am God

Andrew Sloane

'Be still and know that I am God', be still. 'When all things were in quiet silence and night was in the midst of her swift course thine almighty word oh Lord leapt down from thy royal throne.'

Thus the introit for the first Sunday after Christmas Day suggest the spectacularly unspectacular way, in which the word, the second person of the Trinity, slips, as it were, quietly into the world, in the manger at Bethlehem.

Likewise in the story of Easter, we find the disciples making their way quietly in the hush and the semi darkness of the early dawn, to find the stone quietly, even secretly, and quite simply rolled away. The tomb is empty, and without fanfare the risen Lord slips out of the deadly tomb, and in a spectacularly unspectacular way ushers in a whole new way of being and inaugurates nothing less than the new creation.

So too in this Feast of Christ, with the simple unspectacular actions of taking, blessing, breaking and giving bread, and speaking words of deceptive simplicity which in and of themselves can have no power, 'Do this in remembrance of me.' Do this to make me present, the incarnate and risen Lord tabernacles with us, slips in, in the place of nourishment, the manger of this altar, in what has become this House of Bread, in a spectacularly unspectacular way. Here Heaven and Eternity enter our time and space.

Here our stuff is infused with glory, and becomes the vehicle of divinity. Here we become most truly the people and the church that God would have us be. In this meeting of meetings the crucified Lord meets us in the woundedness of our broken lives, and in the tombs, the places of death, in our lives of our own making. His wounded hands touch our wounds, and the wounded healer brings us his healing. Here the risen Lord meets us in those same places and saves us, if we will, from the prisons of being defined by an unredeemed past and offers us instead the ever present possibility of transformation in the hope of resurrection life. Here the ascended Lord meets us in the depths, de profundis, trampling down the gates of hell, and lifting us from the frozen graves of self absorption and death - dealing limitedness to the freeing and limitless vision of our own destiny in him, in the open place of eternal life, that where he is, we might also be and reign with Him in glory. Here not only can we be transformed and made holy. Jesus must not be made by us a prisoner of the tabernacle. But through our graceful witness the world may also be transformed and reordered. So in this feast we are nourished with the life of God himself. As God breathes his very life in the nostrils of the lifeless Adam, so here, and now, he stoops down to give that same kiss of life to the body of the new Adam, the body of Christ, the Church to empower us for mission and ministry in His name in the world. 'Come risen Christ and deign to be our guest.'

Even so, come now, Lord Jesus. Amen